American Criminal Justice

AN INTRODUCTION

Frederick T. Davis

CAMBRIDGE
UNIVERSITY PRESS

CAMBRIDGE
UNIVERSITY PRESS

University Printing House, Cambridge CB2 8BS, United Kingdom

One Liberty Plaza, 20th Floor, New York, NY 10006, USA

477 Williamstown Road, Port Melbourne, VIC 3207, Australia

314–321, 3rd Floor, Plot 3, Splendor Forum, Jasola District Centre, New Delhi – 110025, India

79 Anson Road, #06–04/06, Singapore 079906

Cambridge University Press is part of the University of Cambridge.

It furthers the University's mission by disseminating knowledge in the pursuit of education, learning, and research at the highest international levels of excellence.

www.cambridge.org
Information on this title: www.cambridge.org/9781108493208
DOI: 10.1017/9781108694773

First published 2019

Printed and bound in Great Britain by Clays Ltd, Elcograf S.p.A.

A catalogue record for this publication is available from the British Library.

Library of Congress Cataloging-in-Publication Data
Names: Davis, Frederick T., 1945– author.
Title: American criminal justice : an introduction / Frederick T. Davis.
Description: Cambridge [UK] ; New York, NY : Cambridge University Press, 2019. | Includes bibliographical references and index.
Identifiers: LCCN 2019005625 | ISBN 9781108493208 (hardback)
Subjects: LCSH: Criminal justice, Administration of – United States.
Classification: LCC KF9223 .D39 2019 | DDC 364.973–dc23
LC record available at https://lccn.loc.gov/2019005625

ISBN 978-1-108-49320-8 Hardback
ISBN 978-1-108-71747-2 Paperback

AMERICAN CRIMINAL JUSTICE

American criminal justice may be one of the best known—
and most influential—systems of criminal justice in the world,
but also the least understood: Countless films and television
series portray American police officers, prosecutors, and lawyers, but more than 95 percent of criminal matters result in
guilty pleas, and trials are becoming vanishingly scarce as
people accused of crimes choose to strike deals with increasingly powerful prosecutors. Sentencing "reform" has led to
a burgeoning prison population that is by far the highest
among economically advanced countries. Meanwhile,
American prosecutors have gained increasing (and largely
unchecked) power to apply US criminal laws to worldwide
corporations and individuals with little or no connection with
the country. *American Criminal Justice: An Introduction* provides a readable, comprehensive review of the American
criminal process behind these and other problems.

Frederick T. Davis is Lecturer in Law at the School of Law,
Columbia University, New York, where he teaches courses
on comparative criminal procedures and cross-border crim-
inal investigations. He was a federal prosecutor in the United
States Attorney's Office for the Southern District of New
York, and served as law clerk to Henry J. Friendly, Chief
Judge of the United States Court of Appeals for the Second
Circuit, and Potter Stewart, Justice of the Supreme Court of
the United States. He is a member of the bars of New York
and Paris, is an elected fellow of the American College of
Trial Lawyers and a life member of the American Law
Institute, and was named a chevalier of the National Order
of Merit of France. He lectures frequently at the Ecole
Nationale de la Magistrature, Paris 2, and the Universiteit
van Amsterdam, co-chairs the Business Crime Committee of
the International Bar Association, and has served as a consultant to the prosecutors of the International Criminal Court
and the International Criminal Tribunal for Rwanda.

To Mary, who fights for justice around the world.

CONTENTS

ACKNOWLEDGMENTS

While this book owes much to many, two writers have played a role in its inspiration and deserve mention: one is a good friend; the other I have not met.

The publication in 2003 of *Juger en Amérique et en France* by Antoine Garapon, cowritten with Ionnis Papadopoulos, set a new standard for cross-cultural review of criminal procedures. The book, based in part on the authors spending significant time simply watching American criminal trials, sought not only to understand how US criminal procedures vary so tremendously from French (and other European) ones, but to identify the cultural roots that explain these differences. When I first met him, Antoine mentioned to me, "I am not really a lawyer or jurist; I am sort of an anthropologist of the law." It has been my pleasure to pursue a number of joint projects with Antoine, who as executive director of the Institut des Hautes Etudes sur la Justice in Paris is a veritable one-person think tank on issues relating to criminal justice.

When I set about developing a course on comparative criminal procedures, which I have now taught at Columbia Law School and the University of Amsterdam, I discovered that the academic writing on the subject was (and remains) undeveloped. Among the exceptions to this sparse literature, the most important are the writings of Mirjan R. Damaška, now the Stirling Professor Emeritus at Yale Law School. Many of his major works date from the last century, but no one has captured more elegantly and usefully the many differences between the two great traditions associated with the "common law" of the United States and England and the largely code-based judicial systems of continental Europe.

This book would not have been possible without the talented and energetic contribution of Katie Salvaggio (Columbia JD 2018), who as a student worked ceaselessly on all parts of this book and contributed enormously to it. My friends Sam Bettwy, John D. Gordan, III, Antoine d'Ornano, Charlotte Gunka, Jed S. Rakoff, and Rachel Scott read drafts of the book and provided needed corrections and thoughts. My son Benjamin Davis and his wife Morgan Stewart, who live with criminal justice on a daily basis defending indigent defendants in their jobs at the Federal Defenders Office of San Diego, as well as my wife Mary McGowan Davis, who has served as a defense lawyer, federal prosecutor, judge, teacher, and consultant on a variety of subjects relating to criminal procedures, have contributed immeasurably by responding to frantic questions for updates on current issues. My assistants Linda Orojian and Janine White were heroes in getting the text together.

1 INTRODUCTION

The goal of this book is to provide a general and practical overview of how American criminal justice works for readers who have not studied the subject, and who may not have a background in the American legal system generally. It explores, and tries to explain, some inherently distinctive features of American criminal procedures.

The idea for the book sprang from the May 14, 2011, arrest of Dominique Strauss-Kahn, then the Managing Director of the International Monetary Fund and a likely candidate for the President of France, on charges that he had sexually attacked a chambermaid in the New York hotel where he had been staying. A bit over three months later, the District Attorney of New York submitted a memorandum in court asking that all the charges against him be dismissed. The sequence of procedures between these two events transfixed French readers and television viewers. As a former US federal prosecutor then living in Paris and a member of the Paris Bar, I appeared frequently on French radio and TV to explain the American criminal procedures that were suddenly becoming daily news in France. It was often a challenge, because the first reaction of many was to conclude that procedures that were so difficult to understand must somehow be less fair, that principles of justice so different from their own must somehow be less "just." This experience and others like it led to the development of an academic course on comparative criminal procedures, which I have now taught at the University of Amsterdam and Columbia Law School, and to lectures that I have presented in France at the Ecole Nationale de la Magistrature and Paris 2.

This book focuses on criminal procedures, as distinct from criminal laws; the latter attempt to define what conduct is illegal and worthy of punishment, the former inform us *how* a person suspected or accused of a crime should be treated. These procedures are the core of criminal justice, since they reflect each country's attempt to find the appropriate balance between the interest of the state in punishing (and thus deterring) misconduct, and the right of individuals to maintain their liberty, dignity, and privacy, and to elemental fairness in adjudication. This book will also not discuss **administrative proceedings,** even though they are often linked to criminal ones. In the United States, several agencies in both the federal and in state governments have powers to investigate violations of regulatory laws and to impose financial and other noncustodial sanctions. At the federal level, for example, the **Securities and Exchange Commission** may often investigate violations of federal securities laws and laws related to overseas bribery in parallel with a federal prosecutor. While often appearing similar to criminal proceedings in net result because they cause the imposition of huge fines, administrative proceedings follow their own separate procedures.

Criminal procedures are inevitably linked to national culture and result from each country's distinctive history. Substantive criminal law—the definition of what is illegal—may be converging at least among economically advanced countries; while disagreements about what conduct should be punished sometimes arise, by and large most countries agree on the basic definition of criminal conduct. But the same is much less true with respect to criminal procedures, and observers generally tend to view procedures in countries other than their own as inherently less just than the procedures in which they were trained and that they understand. My belief is that US criminal procedures are no more and no less "fair" and "just" than procedures in other countries; they simply respond to quite different traditions, cultural needs, and expectations.

Differences among national criminal procedures are of growing importance, largely for two reasons: First, crime increasingly takes place across borders; investigators and prosecutors from different countries now work together far more than had been the case previously, and lawyers representing clients—particularly multinational corporations—often face investigations under procedures that are different from those with which they are familiar. In my experience in this area, advising both prosecutors and international corporations on cross-border criminal issues, such efforts are often misguided and ineffective because the participants simply do not understand each other—not just because of language differences, which is itself a big problem, but because the frames of reference, the essential context, of their respective procedures are so different. And second, beginning with the creation of the International Criminal Tribunal for ex-Yugoslavia in 1993, and later the establishment of the International Criminal Court in 2000, there now exist one permanent and occasionally several ad hoc international criminal tribunals that conduct investigations, and have trials, based on **international criminal law** rather than the criminal laws of any one country. But the development of relatively coherent, substantive international criminal law has not been accompanied by the growth of anything that one could call international criminal procedures. As a result, and again based on my experience working with several of those tribunals, I am convinced that most of them work rather inefficiently because their participants are inevitably trained in—and feel comfortable with—the norms and procedures in their home countries, and struggle to understand the mind-set of their colleagues schooled in other traditions.

There is another reason why it is useful to study other countries' criminal procedures, and to take a fresh look at our own through the eyes of others: there is always room for improvement. When I first started studying, and then teaching, criminal procedures on an internationally comparative basis, I hesitated to urge that American criminal procedures could benefit from studying criminal justice systems so different from our own. The idea of simply "grafting" some other country's procedure into one's own seems destined to failure. Indeed, the mixed results at the international criminal tribunals are at least in part a result of such attempts: those tribunals have had neither the time nor the history to grow their own, indigenous procedures; rather, they have created a hodge-podge based as much as anything else on simple negotiation among participants in an effort to maximize the use of their own procedures. But several years of presenting US criminal procedures to non-American audiences—and answering puzzled, sometimes unbelieving, questions about how criminal justice occurs in the

United States—has led me to think that some of those questions deserve attention. Three distinctly American phenomena stand out.

The first is that US criminal justice gives far more unreviewable power to prosecutors than is the case in other countries. In continental Europe, and to some degree in the United Kingdom, as well as in countries whose legal traditions derive from them, a much wider range of decisions by prosecutors is subject to at least some review by a court than is the case in the United States. To some degree, this allows US prosecutors to act more quickly than their counterparts, and often to innovate. To take one example, Chapter 11.D of this book will discuss the rapidly emerging procedure known as the **deferred prosecution agreement,** or "DPA," whereby large corporations can negotiate with a prosecutor to pay (often huge) sums of money but avoid a criminal conviction. Because this procedure is effective (although not free of controversy), some other countries are exploring its use. More insidiously, Chapter 14.B will discuss the relatively recent phenomenon of **mandatory minimum sentences.** While designed to diminish the discretion exercisable by both judges and prosecutors, in fact mandatory minimum provisions provide an unreviewable—and, some believe, pernicious—power to prosecutors that gives them remarkable advantages in negotiating **guilty pleas,** as discussed in Chapter 11.C.

A second distinctly American phenomenon is **discovery,** or more precisely the right and ability of an accused to obtain access to the evidence against him, which is discussed in Chapter 10.B. A US defendant in fact has important rights to such discovery, although those rights are not rigorously codified but rather are spread among a number of laws and rules, as well as interpretations of decades-old **precedent** from the Supreme Court. But what is striking to non-Americans, and worrisome to some in the United States, is that those provisions are largely under the control of *adversaries*—the prosecutor and the defense—who may have a tendency to share no more than the minimum the law clearly requires. Several European and other countries take a different approach: the trial **record** is in essence assembled in advance, and a trial is basically an inquiry whether that record—equally available to both sides—suffices to justify conviction. As a result, "surprises"—and the risk of "trial by ambush"—are greatly diminished.

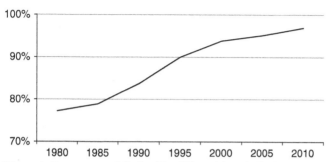

Figure 1: Percentage of Guilty Plea Dispositions in Federal Courts, 1980 to 2010

A further phenomenon may well follow from the first two, at least in part: almost 95 percent of all criminal cases nationwide in the United States—and more than 97 percent of the cases in the federal system—result in a **guilty plea,** where the defendant elects to negotiate with a prosecutor rather than exercise a constitutional right to have the case against him tested by a judge and jury. As recently as 1973, roughly 63 percent of federal criminal cases ended in a guilty plea, with the rest going to trial—a rate roughly comparable to the plea rate in the United Kingdom today. Since then, trials have become less and less frequent. As noted in Figure 1, the rate of guilty pleas has increased relentlessly, and for fiscal year 2017 an official report for the federal courts noted that 97.2 percent of federal defendants pleaded guilty.

More than anything else, this statistic raises eyebrows when I share it with foreign audiences. To many—including this author—the statistic suggests a system that is not working. An analysis of its causes is extremely complex and nuanced, but could appropriately include an appreciation of the many ways in which US criminal justice depends on procedures unique to this country, which seem to make the exercise of the constitutional right to go to trial prohibitively difficult and risky.

Finally, observers of US criminal justice are often struck by some prominent statistical anomalies. Figure 2 shows the number of individuals in prison in the United States, and how that number has mushroomed in the last forty years—that is, during the same period when jury trials in federal cases shrank to less than 3 percent of all criminal cases.

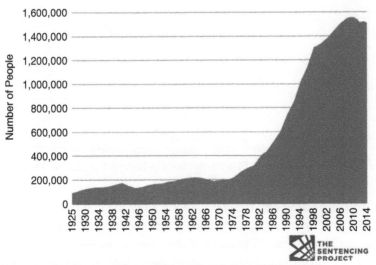

Figure 2: US State and Federal Prison Population, 1925 to 2014

As a result, the prison population as a percentage of overall population, and thus the rate of incarceration, is far higher in the United States
than in any other economically advanced nation:

Further, the racial composition of those caught in the web of criminal prosecutions differs greatly from the population as a whole, since in
most places racial and cultural minorities are disproportionately represented; and of course almost alone among economically advanced
nations, some of the states in the United States (albeit a dwindling
number) exercise the **death penalty**. These very important issues are
beyond the scope of this book, although readers will find in the
Bibliography some of the many excellent books and articles that
address them. But the Conclusion (Chapter 19) argues that these and
other pressing problems with American criminal justice cannot be
understood, or addressed, without first understanding the procedures
in which they have evolved.

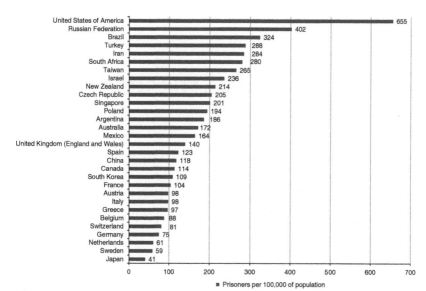

Figure 3: Prison Incarceration Rates in Selected Countries

2 THE FEDERAL STRUCTURE; SOURCES OF THE LAW

A. FEDERAL AND STATE CRIMINAL JUSTICE

Studying criminal justice in the United States is particularly challenging because of the nation's complex structure: the United States is not a unitary jurisdiction but rather a federation of fifty states joined under the terms of the **Constitution** of the United States, and the administration of criminal justice is shared among the federal government and the various states. As a result, one cannot speak of "American criminal law" or "American criminal procedures." Rather, there are fifty-one sets of laws and procedures—one for each state, and one for the federal government. To be sure, the criminal procedures of the various states and of the federal government share many similarities and in general are distinctively different from procedures used in continental Europe and elsewhere, but it is important to remember that the laws, procedures, and practices on any point may differ between one jurisdiction and another.

For reasons of simplicity, this book will mostly focus on criminal procedures in the federal courts of the United States, which are uniform throughout the nation. It will point out some instances where the procedures in various states may differ. But it is well beyond the scope of this book to address such procedures in each of the fifty states, and a reader wishing to dig deeper into the procedures of any specific state will need to consult authorities on that state.

1. The Federal System

Let us begin with a short primer on the constitutional structure of the United States as it applies to lawmaking and criminal justice. Each state is a sovereign that, for purposes of this discussion,

- has its own criminal laws, which may be collected in a "criminal code" or "penal code" of that state (or a differently named equivalent);
- adopts its own criminal procedures, which may be known as a "code of criminal procedures" for that state;
- sets up its own judicial and administrative structures for administering criminal justice within its borders, including police, prosecutors, judges, and courts; and
- develops its own **common law** through the decisions of its courts, which govern criminal procedures in that state.

The federal government is also a sovereign. Federal criminal justice includes the following components:

- Federal criminal laws that are adopted by **Congress** and that create **federal crimes** that can only be prosecuted in federal courts and pursuant to federal criminal procedures. These criminal laws are generally, but not exclusively, found in Title 18 of the United States Code, which is sometimes referred to as the **Federal Criminal Code**, although it is more a compilation of laws adopted over time than a comprehensive code.
- The **Federal Rules of Criminal Procedure**, which apply only to federal proceedings. This book will make frequent reference to these rules, which will be referred to as the "F. R. Crim. P."
- An entire criminal justice system—courts, judges, prosecutors—that is entirely distinct from state analogues. A federal and a state courthouse, for example, can often be found right next to each other in any large city, but are entirely separate.
- Investigative and police agencies that operate nationwide, of which the best known is the **Federal Bureau of Investigation** (FBI).
- Its own common law **precedent**, developed through federal courts, applicable to federal criminal proceedings.

The distinction between state and federal criminal laws can be complicated.

Each state has the inherent power to adopt any criminal laws its legislature deems necessary to protect the welfare of its citizens (subject to review for constitutionality, as noted below). "Everyday" crimes such as theft and murder are generally defined by the criminal laws of the state in which the crime occurs, and are prosecuted under the laws and by the agencies of that state. Most criminal violations implicate only state, and not federal, criminal laws; overall, well over 95 percent of criminal matters occur in state rather than federal courts.

In contrast, the federal government is considered to have **limited powers**: It can only exercise lawmaking, police, and adjudicatory powers in those areas where the Constitution has empowered it to do so; otherwise, at least in theory, all such powers are reserved to the respective states. Thus anyone accused of violating a federal criminal statute can, in principle, demand that the prosecutor demonstrate the source of her power, including the power of Congress to adopt the underlying criminal statute; a federal prosecution not based on an identifiable constitutional mandate may be subject to **dismissal**. In practice, over time, a number of areas have in effect become "federalized," in the sense that most or all law enforcement is handled by federal agencies and in the federal courts, and there is little or no question about their power to act. Interference with or fraud on federal government functions (such as the Post Office and the Treasury), criminal violations of rules established by federal administrative agencies, overseas bribery payments, immigration issues and border protection, counterfeiting, protection of the national securities markets, and certain kinds of terrorism-related activity, for example, are almost exclusively handled by federal authorities.

In some instances, federal laws may be based on "garden variety" criminal activity that is normally the focus of state prosecution but involves acts that cross state or international lines or use interstate mail or wire systems, and is thus constitutionally subject to the power of Congress to criminalize the conduct. Federal prosecutions in such areas are not exclusive of state prosecutions of the same conduct. Narcotics trafficking, for example, can often be prosecuted in either or both a federal and a state court; the federal regulation of banks is sufficiently thorough that both federal and state laws often criminalize conduct related to them. When such **concurrent jurisdiction** exists, there is generally no formal mechanism to allocate whether a given situation will be pursued by federal or state authorities. Rather, the issue is left to the respective police and prosecution authorities to decide. This is generally done on a harmonious and cooperative basis, and in fact federal and state authorities sometimes establish a **joint task force** to investigate crimes together. The preclusive effect of a criminal judgment in one court on an investigation and prosecution in another, known in the United States as **double jeopardy**, is complex, and is addressed in Chapter 12.

A nuanced—but, because of increased globalization, increasingly important—issue is that of **territoriality**: Under what circumstances do American criminal laws apply to conduct taking place outside of the United States, and can such acts be the object of criminal proceedings in United States courts? Until recently, territoriality was mostly a theoretical concern because virtually all criminal matters involved acts taking place within the territory of the prosecuting authority, or at least involved its citizens. Now, however, much crime is organized across borders, and more than one country's police and prosecutorial authorities may assert the power to address the same acts, possibly subjecting a person or company to multiple investigations or prosecutions for the same acts. There is no general federal statute, such as exists in the codes of several European countries, defining the territorial limits under which a person or corporation may be prosecuted in an American court, and the law emerging from court decisions on this issue is in a state of considerable flux. Classically, American prosecutors, and particularly the **Department of Justice**, have been quite aggressive in asserting jurisdiction to prosecute conduct that occurred outside the United States if it was deemed to affect American interests. For example, the Department of Justice has taken the position that a payment in US dollars as part of a crime, even if made outside the United States, can be the basis for a US prosecution simply because of the use of American currency. More recently, however, there has been some movement toward restricting such assertions of territoriality; other than in the area of national security, there is an increasingly enforced presumption that unless Congress has specified that a specific federal legislation was intended to apply to acts occurring outside of the United States, it does not. But the law on this issue is currently evolving, and its parameters are still being tested.

2. The Courts

In the federal judicial system, there are three principal levels of courts:

- **District courts** are trial-level courts, and all federal criminal trials occur there. There are 94 federal **districts** in the United States, each of which fits geographically within one state. Large, populous states may encompass as many as four federal districts; small states may have one.
  - In the state of New York, for example, one finds four of the ninety-four federal districts. The US District Court for the Southern District of New York covers Manhattan and several other counties to its north; the US District Court for the Eastern District of New York—whose courthouse is less than one mile away—covers Brooklyn and other counties mostly to its east. The remaining two federal courts in New York are the US District Court for the Northern District of New York and the US District Court for the Western District of New York.
  - Each district is composed of the federal judges of that district, who are named by the President and must be approved by the Senate. Upon approval, they continue to exercise their judicial powers "during good behavior," which as a practical matter means for life unless they choose to retire or resign. Removal of a federal judge by means of impeachment is complicated and rare. Nationwide there are approximately 650 federal district court judges at any given time. District court judges exercise responsibility in both civil and criminal matters.
  - Each district will also have some **magistrate judges**, who are administratively appointed (and do not, for example, have life tenure as do district court judges). They do not have the powers of district court judges, but rather perform certain tasks subject to review by the actual judges. In the area of criminal justice, they are often delegated significant roles such as conducting **arraignments** upon the arrest of a person, responding to requests for **search** and **arrest warrants** or **wiretap** orders submitted by prosecutors, and trying very minor crimes (known as **misdemeanors**) for which there is no jury trial.
- There are eleven **US courts of appeals** geographically dispersed throughout the United States in regional circuits that encompass several states, plus a separate court of appeals for the District of Columbia circuit (in Washington, DC); there is also a specialized court of appeals for the federal circuit, which considers intellectual property appeals from throughout the United States (and is irrelevant here since it does not review criminal cases). The district courts in New York mentioned previously and those

in several neighboring states fall within the Second Circuit, and appeals from those courts go to the US Court of Appeals for the Second Circuit. Court of appeals judges are also nominated by the President and must be approved by the Senate, and also have life tenure assuming "good behavior." There are approximately 175 federal appellate judges nationwide.

- There is one **Supreme Court of the United States**. It does not entertain **appeals** in the normal sense, because it can decide whether or not to hear a case at all; in fact, the Court decides only about eighty to ninety cases per year, few of which concern criminal matters. Its role is not to review lower court decisions (including criminal ones) to ensure that they were accurately decided, but rather to manage the development of **common law** or **precedent** by interpreting federal criminal laws and procedures in federal cases, and the constitutional principles applicable to federal and state matters. A party that has lost an appeal in a federal court of appeals, or in the highest court of a state, can file a request (called a *certiorari* petition) asking that the Supreme Court review the decision, which the Court either grants (that is, decides to hear the respective parties' arguments and then decide the case on the merits) or not; it generally agrees to hear an appeal only when the lower court decision differs in reasoning from a decision in another federal circuit or a state, thus creating a "conflict" in precedent. Several thousand petitions for *certiorari* are filed with the Supreme Court every year, and thus it selects only a few for review; well over 95 percent of petitions filed with the Court are denied, and thus those decisions are not reviewed at all by the Supreme Court. There are nine Supreme Court Justices, of whom one is specifically appointed (and continues for the remainder of his tenure to serve) as the **Chief Justice of the United States**. As with other federal judges, Supreme Court Justices are named by the President, must be approved by the Senate, and serve for life. The Senate confirmation process for Supreme Court Justices has become increasingly politicized.

Each state organizes its court system as it sees fit. While the nomenclature will vary, there will inevitably be at least one level of trial courts (some states also create "police courts" or other tribunals to hear very minor crimes) and a provision for appellate review. In New York, the principal trial court is confusingly called the Supreme Court, of which there is one in each of the counties of New York; in New York City there are, in addition, Criminal Courts that handle some aspects of criminal matters. Appeals of convictions go to the Appellate Division of the Supreme Court, of which there are four geographically dispersed in the state. The highest court of the state is called the New York Court of Appeals. Some states establish specialized courts for criminal questions; the Texas Court of Criminal Appeals, for example, is the highest court of the state for criminal matters.

Federal courts are not hierarchically superior to state courts in that decisions in state courts are not systematically reviewable in federal courts; the extremely limited power of federal courts to review state court convictions pursuant to a **habeas corpus** petition, known as **collateral review**, will be addressed in Chapter 15.G. The Supreme Court of the United States may review final criminal judgments from the highest court in each state, but only with respect to the conformity of the judgment with the US Constitution or laws (which it does very infrequently through its selective use of the *certiorari* procedure noted previously).

A very simplified structure of the court systems in the federal system and in a hypothetical state one is presented in Figure 4.

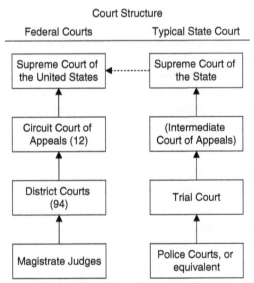

Figure 4: Federal and Typical State Court Structure

B. THE SOURCE OF LAWS AND RULES THAT GOVERN CRIMINAL PROCEDURES

If one asks, "Where do I find the law or procedural rules applicable to a particular stage of a criminal investigation?," the answer is often complicated because neither the federal government nor the various states have systematically codified all the rules applicable to criminal procedure. Rather, depending on the procedural context, one may need to look to one or more of several different sources. As a result, a practitioner in this area must be knowledgeable of, and careful to comply with, a number of legal parameters, which differ among the various states and the federal government—an often daunting challenge for those not used to researching American law. And even within one or another court system, entirely different types or sources of laws and procedures may be applicable at different stages of the matter.

This book will explore the sequential steps of a criminal matter, at each of which quite different kinds of legal rules may apply:

- *The investigation* includes police activity to determine if a crime was committed, to identify the person or persons responsible for a crime, and to assemble evidence upon which a prosecution may be based. In the federal system, there is no single code that sets out the requirements for an investigation, although a number of federal laws bear on them. As noted in Chapter 3.C and 4, there is no systematic judicial role during an investigation. More generally, there are no specific procedural requirements for the conduct of an investigation unless and until the prosecutor in her discretion elects to prosecute, as set forth in the next bullet. For example, the police or the prosecutor may commence and conduct an investigation without any judicial input or formal step; they later may simply choose to stop investigating, and generally need to make no formal account or record of this decision, or seek review of it from a judge. The police largely proceed on their own, and at the beginning of an investigation may coordinate with prosecutors somewhat informally. Often the only times during an investigation when formal, codified rules come into play is when a prosecutor may in certain limited and specific instances need to turn to a judge to obtain court authorization to take investigative steps that threaten a person's liberty (arrest) or privacy (search, wiretap). This is explored in Chapter 4.C.

Many important principles governing police conduct are not found in codes or written rules at all, but are found in judicial decisions, or **precedent**, which have interpreted certain provisions in the Constitution to set limits on police conduct, particularly with respect to custodial interrogations, searches of persons or premises, or seizures of property that threaten individual liberty or privacy (see Chapter 4). The enforcement of these principles often occurs through exercise of an **exclusionary rule** prohibiting the use at trial of illegally obtained evidence, rather than through judicial or administrative review of police conduct during an investigation; exclusionary rules are discussed in greater detail in Chapter 10.C.

- *The charging decision*, which is the decision by a prosecutor whether or not to accuse a person or company of one or more violations of a criminal statute, is not governed by rule or statute at all. As discussed in Chapter 6.A, in the federal system a prosecutor has virtually unreviewable discretion whether or not to prosecute; no rule or statute addresses that issue, and there is no general avenue for judicial review of it. The federal **Department of Justice** has in some instances published **guidelines** on how it exercises its discretion. These public guidelines are often useful (and are thus an important "source" of strategic input), but they are often quite vague and in any event not "binding" on the prosecution. If a prosecutor decides to prosecute, she can obtain an **indictment** to formally charge the accused only with the approval of a **grand jury**, as discussed in Chapter 6.B. Some rules regarding conduct before a grand jury are found in the F. R. Crim. P. But grand jury procedural rules basically address issues concerning their composition and conduct; they do not provide a framework to evaluate a prosecutor's decision to prosecute (or not), and that decision is generally not reviewed by a judge. State rules vary, and not all states require a grand jury; but in general, there is no specific standard or rule for the exercise of prosecutorial discretion.

- *The pretrial phase* consists of activity after a defendant has been accused—generally by the issuance of an indictment—and before trial commences. Once a prosecutor has obtained an indictment in federal court, the case becomes active (and is assigned a formal judicial **docket** number) and is systematically supervised by one or more judges. Some rules relating to the pretrial phase are found in the F. R. Crim. P., but many important details are left to each judge to manage. The **Speedy Trial Act**, discussed in Chapter 10.A, governs time periods during which a case must proceed to trial. The defendant's access to evidence or information held by the prosecutor (known as **discovery** and discussed in Chapter 10.B) is governed by a mixture of several different kinds of rules, some appearing in federal legislation, some in the F. R. Crim. P., and some in **precedent** established by Supreme Court decisions and interpretations of that precedent by the lower courts. Some kinds of federal **negotiated outcomes** (particularly **guilty pleas**) are covered in detail by the F. R. Crim. P. (see Chapter 11.C); other increasingly important procedures—such as **deferred prosecution agreements** and **non-prosecution agreements**—are not codified at all, but have developed through practice and court decisions. See Chapter 11.D.

- *The trial.* Some of the F. R. Crim. P. apply to federal trials, but many important questions concerning the conduct of trials are not found in those rules but rather are left to tradition, practice, and the discretion of the judge; further, certain principles elaborated through precedent by the Supreme Court and other courts apply to the trial. The applicable **rules of evidence**—which in federal courts are mostly codified in the **Federal Rules of Evidence**—govern many but not all issues relating to the **admissibility** of evidence; in addition, evidence may be restricted by the application of **exclusionary rules** developed by the Supreme Court and other courts. Several important attributes of a trial—such as rights to counsel, rights to cross-examine, and certain elements of jury deliberations—have been addressed by the Supreme Court as a matter of constitutional interpretation. See Chapter 13.F.

- *Sentencing* issues in federal courts are addressed in part in the F. R. Crim. P., but even more important are the **Federal Sentencing Guidelines,** which provide the matrix upon which federal judges decide and impose sentences (see Chapter 14.B). State courts will have their own, and often very different, procedures and standards for the imposition of sentences.

- *Appeals.* The mechanics of filing and pursuing an appeal in the federal system are governed by the **Federal Rules of Appellate Procedure,** and the court of appeals for each circuit may have its own rules concerning certain details. Important questions regarding the scope of appellate review, however, can only be determined by reviewing Supreme Court and other court decisions, as well as tradition. These are discussed in Chapter 15. The Supreme Court has adopted its own **Rules of the Supreme Court,** which govern the mechanics of procedures in that Court. Each state organizes its appeals procedure differently.

- *Collateral review* refers to possible review of a criminal conviction after an appeal, which is limited and infrequent. In the federal system, the procedures for such review are largely, but not entirely, set forth in legislation. In some instances, a review of a criminal conviction may itself be a civil proceeding and may be governed by the **Federal Rules of Civil Procedure** (see Chapter 15.G).

It is important to understand that the sources described here mostly relate to criminal matters that take place in federal courts and have no bearing on state investigations and trials, which are governed by a generally similar but often distinct array of rules and laws specific to each state. The Bibliography will identify the principal texts applicable to the federal system, as well as those in the state of New York. Note that each of the other states will have similar but not identical texts and sources of authorities. And in both federal and state prosecutions, extremely important principles may not appear in written laws at all, but only in judicial precedent, which may vary from circuit to circuit within the federal court system, as well as from state to state.

This book will not address the criminal procedures applicable to **juveniles**, almost all of which take place in state rather than federal courts. Each state enacts its own procedures to deal with the complex issues that arise when a young person is suspected of committing or being involved in a criminal offense. Among the elements that may vary from state to state is the age at which young people are in fact treated differently from adults, the length (and form) of incarceration that is deemed appropriate, and whether usual components of a criminal trial, such as a jury and complex rules of evidence, will be used. The book will also not deal with **military** justice, which follows entirely different laws, rules, and procedures.

As this summary shows, identifying the laws, rules, precedent, and practices applicable to any specific point in a criminal matter can be a complicated exercise. A lawyer confronted with a specific procedural challenge must be aware that there is a wide variety of potential sources that may apply, which will vary considerably depending on the exact stage of the process as well as the local law. This is inherently because the United States not only is committed to a **common law**, and not a code-based legal system, but is a federation with a complicated allocation of powers among the federal authority and the various states.

3 INVESTIGATION AND EVIDENCE-GATHERING—THE PARTICIPANTS

A. THE POLICE

Most criminal investigations are initiated by police, either acting reactively in immediate response to a situation (*in flagrante*) or proactively in the absence of an immediate need for police intervention. At the federal level, there are several specialized police agencies, including the **Federal Bureau of Investigation** (FBI), the Drug Enforcement Agency, the Secret Service (which is tasked with protecting the President but also with investigating counterfeiting), and the Bureau of Alcohol, Tobacco, Firearms, and Explosives. Most investigative federal agencies report directly or indirectly to the **Attorney General of the United States**, who heads the **Department of Justice**. Each state organizes its own police functions as it sees fit. Counties, cities, or small towns within a state may have police forces that may range in scale from the New York City Police Department, composed of approximately twenty thousand officers, to a village that may have one policeman. While some state law enforcement officials are locally elected, federal officers are not. Although they investigate and enforce different bodies of laws (see Chapter 2.A.1), federal and state police authorities generally coordinate harmoniously, either informally or through so-called **joint task forces**.

Police officers do not require authorization from a prosecutor or judge in order to commence an investigation, whether reactively in response to an *in flagrante* event or proactively. While the police may well create an internal administrative record of an investigation, no judicial record is generally created until there has been an arrest or formal accusation. The police possess broad powers to investigate crimes that **victims** or other individuals bring to their attention, although victims have no formal role in an investigation and do not have the legal means to compel an investigation (see Chapter 13.J).

Police officers generally do coordinate with prosecutors, often informally, for two practical reasons. *First,* there are a number of investigative tools for which the explicit permission of a judge is necessary to protect the liberty or privacy of the person involved; these include wiretaps, searches of premises, seizures of objects or data, and arrests other than *in flagrante.* To do this, the police will ask a prosecutor to apply to a judge for an appropriate order, such as an **arrest warrant,** a **search warrant,** or a **wiretap order,** usually on the basis that there is **probable cause** to believe that a crime has been committed and that the proposed order will lead to the discovery of evidence of the crime (see Chapter 4. C). *Second,* because the ultimate decision whether to prosecute will be made by the prosecutor (see Chapter 6.B), police officers will coordinate with the relevant prosecutor's office on the status of the investigation, will take guidance as to whether further investigation is needed in order to prove a case, and will cooperate in the presentation of evidence to a **grand jury** as needed and ultimately in the presentation of proof at trial.

The police typically memorialize their work in memoranda that they share with the prosecutor. However, such memoranda are not the equivalent of a *procès verbal* in the French system, and will not be considered **admissible evidence** of guilt at a trial, due to **rules of evidence** that ban the use of **hearsay** (see Chapter 13.E). Administrative review of police conduct varies considerably among state and federal jurisdictions. Victims of police abuse may have opportunities to seek compensation through administrative proceedings or civil suits, and abuse perceived to be systemic is sometimes addressed through civil class actions brought by victims. Most violations of police conduct norms in specific criminal cases are addressed through the court's **exclusion** at trial of evidence obtained in violation of the Constitution or other laws, discussed in Chapters 10.C and 13.E.

B. THE PROSECUTOR

The role of a prosecutor is relatively informal during the early stages of many investigations, particularly those initiated by police. In some cases, proactive investigations may be initiated in the first instance by the prosecutor; in the federal system, for example, a prosecutor may be named as **special counsel** to look into a specific problem, and any prosecutor can decide to investigate a matter and turn to the relevant police agency for help in doing so. As a practical matter, coordination between the police and prosecutor is always critical because the prosecutor alone controls the decision of whether or not to prosecute, as noted in Chapter 6.A. As noted in Chapter 4.C, the prosecutor is also essential in obtaining court orders for investigative tools like arrest warrants, wiretaps, and searches.

Prosecutors are not members of the judiciary but rather are lawyers with the same legal training as defense counsel, judges, and in-house counsel; they must be members of the local bar and are subject to its professional obligations (see Chapter 18). Although the post of being a prosecutor is generally a full-time job (some very small state jurisdictions may use prosecutors hired on a part-time basis), many prosecutors either were or later become private attorneys, in-house counsel, or judges, and changes among such positions are common. There is no procedure for a private prosecutor to represent a **victim** in a criminal proceeding. State prosecutors are often locally elected. The senior federal prosecutor for each federal **district**, known as the **US Attorney**, is appointed by the President for a term of four years; by tradition, US Attorneys resign upon the election of the new president. US Attorneys are part of the **Department of Justice** and report to the **Attorney General of the United States**. Each US Attorney appoints her staff on a nonpolitical basis; they are known as **Assistant US Attorneys** ("AUSAs"). Some AUSAs spend their careers as prosecutors; many others serve for a period of years—often to gain trial experience—and then move to other positions in the profession.

C. THE JUDICIAL FUNCTION DURING AN INVESTIGATION

In the United States, there is no equivalent of an **investigating magistrate** that characterizes some European systems, and judges in fact have no systematic role in criminal investigations at all. They have no voice in the decision whether or not to prosecute, which is made solely by a prosecutor (see Chapter 6.A), and in the federal and most state systems, this decision cannot be reviewed by a judge. While, as noted, a judge may be asked to authorize specific interventions that affect personal liberty—such as wiretaps, seizure of evidence, entry into premises, and nonurgent arrests—a judge who approves such a request does not thereby supervise the overall investigation, or even have a comprehensive understanding of it. Judges become systematically involved in a criminal case only after the **arrest** or **indictment** of an individual. At that point, there will for the first time be a judicial **docket** in the court file where formal records relating to the individual's case will be kept. The docket will be assigned to a judge or a chamber of judges, who are often asked in the first instance to determine conditions of liberty of someone who has been arrested, and who generally supervise a case as it proceeds to trial (see Chapter 10.C).

D. THE DEFENSE FUNCTION DURING AN INVESTIGATION

A person or company being investigated does not have a specific status or identifiable rights as such, even if he or it becomes a clear target of the investigation, and in the federal system at least does not receive official notice of the investigation or have any opportunity to make a formal intervention in it. In the federal system (some state procedures differ on this point), neither a person subject to investigation nor his attorney has a right to be consulted prior to a decision to prosecute; they also do not have access to evidence obtained by the police or presented to a **grand jury** or a right to insist on being heard by the grand jury.

That said, as a practical matter, individuals and companies often learn that they are the object of an investigation either by hearing of activity by police (who may be interviewing witnesses) or by receiving a **subpoena** to testify before a grand jury or an administrative agency, and may retain an attorney to prepare for a possible defense. (While a person without funds has a right to have an attorney appointed once he is either arrested or formally accused, there is no right to an appointed attorney prior to one of those events, so pre-arrest/accusation defense efforts can only be accomplished by persons or companies with funds to retain an attorney.) An attorney representing a person or company being investigated can actively engage in her own investigation to prepare for adversarial discussions with a prosecutor or for trial, even before formal charges exist. An attorney may interview prospective fact witnesses, hire experts, and begin the process of developing a defensive strategy. In many instances where an attorney is advising a person under investigation, she will at least evaluate whether to contact the prosecutor. One advantage of doing so is that once it is clear that a person is represented by an attorney, neither the prosecutor nor the police should interview that person without informing the attorney. A lawyer may also evaluate whether it is in the strategic interest of the client to explore the possibility of a negotiated outcome, since as noted in Chapter 11 such discussions can take place at any time, even before a formal accusation. In conducting an investigation, an attorney must be careful not to influence or suborn the testimony of prospective witnesses (which could lead to prosecution for **obstruction of justice**), although there is generally less concern of an accusation of obstructing justice than is the case in Europe, and as a result attorneys tend to be fairly active during the pretrial process. Her efforts are generally protected by two privileges: the **attorney/client privilege** and the **work product privilege** (see Chapter 18.B).

Any person who is arrested, or subject to deprivation of liberty in order to be questioned, has a right to be represented by an attorney and to be informed of this right, and to have an attorney appointed by a court to represent him if he does not have the funds to retain an attorney. (**Right to counsel** issues will be discussed in greater detail in Chapter 9.A.) At an arrest or custodial interrogation, if the person interrogated asks for the appointment of an attorney because he lacks the funds to hire one, an attorney will not be appointed at the interrogation itself (which, under the precedent of the *Miranda v. Arizona* decision, should cease upon invocation of the right to counsel by the interviewee); instead, appointment of counsel, if needed, generally happens at **arraignment**, when a person is brought before a court for the first time (see Chapter 9.A). More broadly, however, anyone involved in a criminal investigation—even a witness who is not under arrest and does not consider himself at risk of being charged—may out of nervousness or concern for unknown risks choose to have a privately retained attorney present during an interview or in response to any aspect of an investigation; and other than in a **grand jury** (where a lawyer may not be physically present, although she can be just outside the grand jury room), neither the police nor a prosecutor can ask that a lawyer be excluded. Such a person does not, however, have a right to have an attorney appointed at state expense unless he is formally accused, arrested, or otherwise deprived of liberty.

4 INVESTIGATION AND EVIDENCE-GATHERING— PROCEDURES

Police investigations have two principal and overlapping functions in the administration of criminal justice: (1) to *determine if a crime occurred* (and if so to *identify* and, when appropriate, arrest the person or persons responsible); and (2) to *collect evidence* that would be **admissible** at trial and sufficient to prove the guilt of those ultimately accused of responsibility. The length and complexity of this process, and the range of investigative techniques brought to bear, vary tremendously. In a very simple "street crime," an apparent culprit may be identified and arrested immediately on a reactive basis, and the evidence-gathering may be straightforward and limited in scope; investigations in more complicated matters may take place on a proactive basis and can take months or even years in order to review and obtain evidence before a decision can be made to prosecute. This chapter will review the principal steps or procedures that may come into play in a variety of circumstances. The discussion will be divided into four topics: (A) the distinction between reactive investigations precipitated by an on-the-spot arrest and proactive ones where the arrest follows an investigation; (B) evidence-gathering techniques that may be employed *by the police without any judicial authorization*; (C) those instances where prior *judicial approval* is necessary; and (D) the use of a *grand jury* during an investigation.

A. PRE-ARREST AND POST-ARREST INVESTIGATIONS

Figures 5 and 6 show the principal stages of an investigation and subsequent steps in the criminal process through trial and appeal.

There are two such illustrations because the first steps generally fall into two fairly distinct categories:

- In many relatively simple cases, as summarized in Figure 5, the precipitating event is the arrest of a person on a reactive basis, often one caught *in flagrante* during or immediately after the apparent commission of a crime. In that circumstance, the evidence gathering occurs as part of or after the arrest, and usually with significant time constraints mandated by an arrestee's right to a **speedy trial** (see Chapter 10.A). Once there has been an arrest, there will be a judicial **docket** established and a judge or judges will supervise the path toward a trial or other disposition. Even under these circumstances, however, the police and the prosecutors may continue to investigate and obtain evidence without systematic recourse to a judge, as noted in the next section. But the existence of an arrest means that the person arrested will upon **arraignment** be formally represented by an attorney, including one appointed to represent him if he lacks funds, who may attempt to be active in her own investigation and preparation, as noted in Chapter 3.D.
- In more complex cases, summarized in Figure 6, an arrest is not made until after the police, working closely with a prosecutor, have proactively obtained and reviewed evidence, and the prosecutor has made a decision to prosecute and often has obtained an **indictment**. During a preaccusation/prearrest phase, the police and prosecutor may need to obtain approval from a judge for certain investigative procedures, but this is done secretly and unilaterally; in fact, the person the government is investigating may not have been arrested or even have any knowledge of the investigation, and thus may or may not have counsel at this stage.

The sources of the rules that govern such investigations are particularly complex. As noted in Chapter 2.B, there is no comprehensive code or written set of rules that systematically sets forth all of the procedures relevant to a police investigation. In fact, many of the most important legal parameters of criminal investigations are not set out in formal laws or rules but have been established by decisions of the Supreme Court interpreting the US Constitution. In particular, the **Fourth Amendment** to the Constitution, which protects "[t]he right of the people to be secure in their persons, houses, papers, and effects," has been interpreted to establish certain rules to protect privacy and related personal rights; the **Fifth Amendment** protects against **double jeopardy** and compelled **self-incrimination**; the **Sixth Amendment**

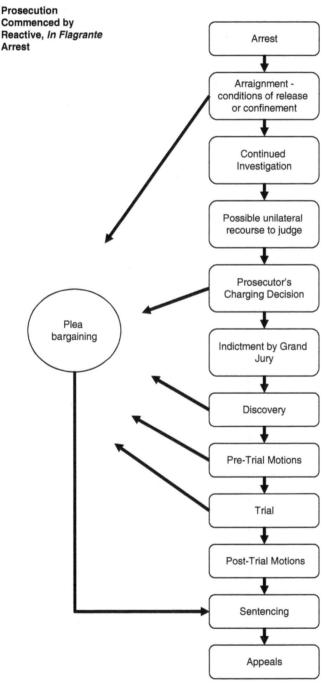

Figure 5: Steps in a Prosecution—Reactive

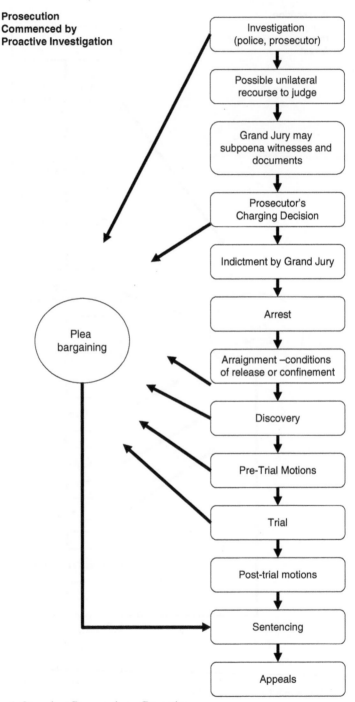

Figure 6: Steps in a Prosecution—Proactive

protects the rights to a public **jury trial**, the **right to counsel**, and the right to **confront** adverse witnesses; and the **Eighth Amendment** protects against "excessive bail," "excessive fines," and "cruel and unusual punishments." Many of these provisions are primarily enforced through **exclusionary rules**, judge-created rules that evidence taken in violation of certain constitutional or other rights will be excluded—that is, not received as evidence—at trial, generally on a theory that this is the best way of deterring improper police or other official conduct (see Chapter 13.E).

In very general terms, judicial decisions interpreting these and other parts of the Constitution establish the following principles:

- A person's liberty cannot be restrained by arrest unless there is **probable cause** to believe that he has committed a crime and the existence of such probable cause has been determined by a judge prior to the restraint (who can authorize an arrest by issuing an **arrest warrant**). A judicially issued arrest warrant is not required if obtaining one would risk flight or danger to others, in which case a warrantless *in flagrante*, on-the-spot arrest can be made.
- A person under arrest or restraint is deemed to be in an inherently adversarial situation and cannot be **interrogated** absent compliance with certain rules designed to respect his rights to remain silent and to be advised by an attorney, by making sure he is informed of them.
- A person's privacy (such as the sanctity of his home, his personal effects, or his communications) cannot be invaded unless the police first obtain a judicial **search warrant** or **wiretap order** from a judge, after establishing **probable cause** to believe that a crime has occurred and that the evidence being sought will bear on it.

Police investigative techniques will generally be circumscribed by procedures designed to protect these judicially elaborated rights.

B. POLICE INVESTIGATION WITHOUT JUDICIAL INTERVENTION

When apprised of facts showing that a crime has been committed, and without any prior authorization by a judge or the prosecutor, the police may set about investigating the crime using a wide range of police techniques. These may include inspecting crime scenes and taking custody of physical evidence; surveillance, such as following suspects and taking photographs; obtaining evidence from public sources; and conducting scientific analyses and forensic evaluations, such as a review of fingerprints, DNA, or handwriting. In complex cases involving multiple jurisdictions (within the United States or internationally), the police may coordinate—formally or informally—with their counterparts in other jurisdictions.

Police officers may interview witnesses who agree to be interviewed. If a potential witness (whether or not a suspect) refuses to meet with or be interviewed by the police, the police cannot force him to do so, and there is no common judicial procedure to compel a police interview; it is in such situations that a prosecutor may obtain a grand jury **subpoena** to compel the witness to appear and testify before a **grand jury**, as described in Chapter 6.B. (As noted in the Introduction, there are entirely different procedures applicable to **administrative proceedings**—such as those led by the **Securities and Exchange Commission** in matters relating to securities matters—and both state and federal administrators may have the ability to compel testimony.)

On the other hand, federal laws and the laws of some states make it a crime to lie to a police officer, even in a voluntary interview. In 2004, for example, businesswoman and TV personality Martha Stewart was convicted, under 18 U.S.C. § 1001, of lying to an FBI officer when she consented to be interviewed about certain sales of stock, and she served five months in prison even though she was never charged with any crime relating to the facts about which she was interviewed. At the end of a police interview, it is not common practice for the police to ask the interviewee to sign a statement unless they suspect that the person is responsible for a crime, in which case they often ask the person to sign a document that amounts to a **confession** and will be intended to be received as such in a trial. In most instances where the police interview a witness who is not a suspect, the officer will generally write a careful memorandum of the interview, which becomes part of the file available to the prosecutor to review in determining whether or not to prosecute. Because of the **rules of evidence** applicable at trials, and especially the rule generally prohibiting **hearsay**, a memorandum by a police officer or even a written statement adopted and signed by a witness is not admissible at trial as evidence against the accused. (But a statement by the accused himself, if taken appropriately, is admissible against him as a confession.)

In certain kinds of long-running criminal activity, particularly involving gangs or other large groups, the police may engage in an **undercover investigation**, either when a police agent infiltrates a gang by impersonating a crook or by working with an **accomplice** who has agreed to cooperate with authorities, often as part of a plea negotiation, as discussed in Chapter 11.C. Both an undercover police officer and a cooperating accomplice may "wear a wire"—that is, carry a secret electronic device to record conversations. Unlike **wiretaps**, discussed in Section C, a recording conducted with the consent of one of the participants does not need authorization by a judge.

When the police interrogate someone who is under arrest or whose liberty is otherwise restrained, the situation is inherently adversarial because their interests are diametrically opposed; yet it is also one-sided because the police are by definition professionals and the person interrogated not only is unlikely to be aware of the relevant risks and rights, but generally will not be advised by an attorney. Further, the police often are vastly better informed about the facts than the person being questioned. In 1966, the Supreme Court announced rules (called *Miranda* **warnings**, after the decision *Miranda v. Arizona*) that, while frequently modified since then, set out the basic protocol for a **custodial interrogation**, where a person is either arrested or under sufficient restraint that he genuinely feels he is not free to leave. Under those circumstances, and absent unusual exigencies such as a fast-moving emergency, the police cannot interrogate the witness—and if they do, any fruits of the interrogation risk being excluded at trial—unless they first inform him that he has a right to remain silent, that if he chooses to speak anything he says may be used against him, that he has the right to an attorney, and that if he does not have funds to pay for an attorney, one will be provided at state expense. If after hearing these warnings the witness voluntarily **waives** his rights and agrees to proceed, then his statements will generally be admissible in a trial against him; but if he states that he does not wish to speak, or that he wants to confer with an attorney, then the interrogation should stop, and anything said thereafter would risk **exclusion** as evidence at trial. For

obvious reasons, police officers are eager to obtain **confessions** from
those they consider responsible for a crime, and custodial interrogations
are often "cat and mouse" affairs where the police attempt to persuade
the person being interrogated to waive his rights. The **admissibility** of
such confessions—whether in the form of a document signed by the
person himself, a video recording of the interrogation, or an oral confession about which a police officer testifies at trial—thus depends on the
care with which the interrogating officer administers the *Miranda* warnings. Officers will often ask the interviewee to sign a document stating
that he has been informed of his *Miranda* warnings, and some jurisdictions require that such interrogations be recorded by videotape to insure
a proper record of exactly what happened. The circumstances of
a custodial interrogation leading to a confession are often explored
pretrial in an **evidentiary hearing** if the defendant against whom such
evidence is offered contests the procedures used relating to the confession by making a **motion to suppress** it at trial (see Chapter 10.C).

When a police officer effects a legal **arrest** of a person—whether
with or without a warrant—they may then search him **incident to the
arrest**. The validity of the search incident to arrest may thus depend on
whether the arrest itself was legal—that is, whether the arresting officer
either had an appropriately issued **arrest warrant**, or if the arrest was
made on the basis that the police had **probable cause** to believe that
the person committed a crime *and* the circumstances did not permit
resort to a judge because of a risk of flight. A search incident to arrest
may include a full search of the arrestee, including any containers he
has on his person. However, if they find a cell phone or other form of
data storage on the person of the arrestee, they generally cannot
"search" it for data or messages found on it, but must obtain
a separate **search warrant** to do so. A search incident to an arrest
must be limited to the area of "immediate control" in which the arrestee
could reach for a weapon or destroy evidence. If an arrest occurs in
a house, the officer cannot justifiably search other rooms beyond where
the arrest took place, or search through desk drawers in the room itself;
such spaces are not "incident to the arrest." On the other hand, even
without reasonable suspicion, an officer may look into closets and other
spaces immediately connected to the place of arrest as a precaution to
ensure his safety from an unexpected attack. If a person is arrested

while a driver or a passenger in a car, the police need not obtain a warrant to search the entire car if they have probable cause to believe it contains evidence of a crime, and in any event may search the immediate area around the person arrested. Self-evidently, many inquiries into the legality of such searches (and thus the **admissibility** of any evidence seized) may involve difficult "line drawing" to distinguish between legal and illegal searches, although there is a tendency among judges to give police agents the benefit of doubts if it appears that an officer was acting in good faith.

Judges defer to police agents' judgment in searches

The key requirement underlying *any* arrest is the requirement of **probable cause**, which the person arrested can contest prior to trial via an **exclusionary rule** if evidence seized incident to the arrest is offered against him. During an **evidentiary hearing** held in response to a defendant's **motion to suppress** such evidence, the trial court will review the objective information available to an officer who conducted an arrest without a warrant to evaluate whether the information amounted to probable cause; if the arrest was pursuant to an arrest warrant issued (on an *ex parte* basis) by another judge, a trial judge could in theory find that the prior judge erred and that insufficient facts to show probable cause had been shown, but in fact, trial judges tend to give a strong presumption of regularity to such prior determinations. In any event, the fact that incriminating evidence was in fact found in a search incident to arrest cannot be used to justify the arrest or the incident search.

ex No post reasoning

The police have much greater flexibility to conduct **border searches** at or near national boundaries or their functional equivalents, such as international airports. Police generally do not need a warrant to search the person of someone entering the country, but must act "reasonably" in the context of the basis for suspicion and the scope of their search.

Relate to cell phones too?

Even if a police officer lacks a probable cause basis to arrest someone, if she can point to "specific and articulable facts" indicating the person may be involved in a crime, she may briefly stop and detain the person and subject him to a "pat down" search (often called a *frisk*) to ensure that the person is not carrying a dangerous weapon, and may arrest the person if sufficient incriminating information is then found during the frisk. Many narcotics arrests begin in this fashion.

The practice of **stop and frisk** is controversial because some officers may conduct the stops in a discriminatory manner. In 2013, a federal court in New York found that the New York City Police Department (NYPD) was responsible for an unconstitutional pattern and practice of racial profiling in executing such stops; the NYPD is now subject to monitoring as it undergoes reform. See *Floyd v. City of New York*, 770 F.3d 1051 (2d Cir. 2014).

C. JUDICIAL INTERVENTION IN A CRIMINAL INVESTIGATION

The police activities described so far generally occur without any prior judicial approval, supervision, or participation. Under certain circumstances, especially where individual liberty or privacy is concerned, neither the police nor the prosecutor can proceed without obtaining approval from a judge. Such judicial interventions are *ex parte*, secret, and unilateral in the sense that they are not subject to contest by, or even notice to, the person who may be affected; they are limited to their specific context, and do not involve a judge in any other aspect of the investigation or give a judge any general supervisory role in it. Because the decisions are made without input from an adversary, if the fruits of such an investigation are later offered at trial, the person against whom the evidence is offered has an opportunity to demonstrate that the intervention occurred without sufficient evidentiary support or in breach of the applicable procedures, in which case the evidence seized thereby may be **excluded** at trial (see Chapter 10.C).

Some of the principal areas where judicial intervention is necessary during an investigation are as follows:

- *Arrest.* Prior to an **indictment**, if a suspect is not apprehended *in flagrante* and where there is no risk of flight, the police cannot conduct an arrest without an **arrest warrant** signed by a judge. Under these circumstances, the prosecutor will typically ask a judge for the issuance of such a warrant based upon a sworn **affidavit** from a police officer attesting to evidence showing probable cause that the person to be arrested is responsible for a crime. Once a grand jury has issued an **indictment**, an arrest warrant may be automatically issued on the ground that probable cause has already been established. A prosecutor may ask that an indictment and arrest warrant be **sealed**, which means that they are not public until the indicted person is arrested. Once issued, the warrant may be executed by a police officer in any place where the person is found. Warrants are often disseminated through police networks, and police sometimes publicize them, including through news outlets and other media, to seek help from the public in finding the person they are looking for. A person arrested in a different state from the one seeking his arrest will be subject to streamlined **extradition** procedures—far simpler than extradition procedures applicable internationally (discussed later in this section), and individuals apprehended on an out-of-state arrest warrant do not often contest extradition to the issuing state. Upon arrest, the police may conduct a search of the person **incident to arrest,** as described in Section B.

- *Wiretaps.* Under the "one party consent" rule, a police officer or a private person who is herself a party to a telephone or other conversation may record it without judicial permission, but the police may not use wiretaps or hidden devices to record telephone or other private conversations among non-consenting participants without a formal **wiretap order**. Under federal legislation addressed to "Wire and Electronic Communications Interceptions and Interceptions of Oral Communications," 18 U.S.C. § 2510 *et seq.*, which applies to both federal and state investigations (an unusual instance of federal legislation applying to state procedures), obtaining a wiretap order involves careful scrutiny by a judge of the grounds justifying an application, which must demonstrate **probable cause** that a serious crime has been committed or is being committed (the legislation lists the specific federal crimes that suffice for this purpose, although analogous state crimes also suffice). The application must demonstrate why "other [presumably less intrusive] investigative procedures" have been tried and failed or "reasonably appear unlikely to succeed." The wiretap order must contain careful procedures for "minimization" of nonpertinent communications and to avoid conversations with attorneys that might be covered by the **attorney/client privilege;** and must have a relatively short duration (no longer than 30 days) requiring frequent renewal. The **Foreign Intelligence Surveillance Act** provides special procedures for wiretaps involving foreign sources.
- *Search and seizure.* Absent **consent** of the owner or resident (which police may seek in the first instance if they believe it will be effective and not result in flight or the destruction of evidence), or **hot pursuit,** where the police chase a person known to have committed a crime into

a building in order to arrest him and then search him incident to that arrest as set forth previously, the **Fourth Amendment** has been interpreted to require that police cannot enter or search a home, office, or other nonpublic place without a **search warrant** signed by a judge on the basis of a showing by the police that specifies the premises to be searched and demonstrates **probable cause** that evidence of a crime will be found there. In the federal system, the procedures for obtaining a search warrant are set forth in Rule 41 of the Federal Rules of Criminal Procedure. When investigators determine that they need access to a place in order to obtain evidence (and after consent has been refused, or is considered to be unlikely or may cause flight), the prosecutor will present to a judge a request for a search warrant, generally based on an **affidavit** by a police officer demonstrating the factual basis for determining probable cause. The judge will consider, and rule on, this application in secret. Officers armed with a signed warrant usually execute a "knock and announce" search, alerting the owner of their presence and waiting several seconds to allow an occupant to answer before entering with force. To justify a "no-knock" entry, police must have a reasonable suspicion that knocking would be dangerous, futile, or lead to the destruction of evidence.

The law recognizes the home as a specially protected enclave where citizens should enjoy a reasonable expectation of privacy. In *Florida v. Jardines*, the Supreme Court extended the notion of the home to the front porch and areas "immediately surrounding and associated with the home" for Fourth Amendment purposes (569 U.S. 1 [2013]). Defining boundaries is challenging for social guests, tenants, and other borderline cases, but the law generally aims to protect life at home from government intrusion.

- *Data.* The law recognizes a privacy interest in digital information. For example, while the police may seize a cell phone found on a person they arrest, they generally must obtain a **search warrant** before gaining access to the information stored on it. The police are increasingly confronted with potentially incriminating information that is stored on cell phones or other places under a strong form of encryption. The law is at present quite unsettled whether carriers or hardware manufacturers must cooperate with law enforcement officers in their efforts to decrypt such information. Further, at least under some circumstances, a person cannot be forced to provide the password for her stored data, since doing so under compulsion might amount to **self-incrimination**, protected by the **Fifth Amendment.** If the data constituting personal communications such as emails are held by a service provider, the **Stored Communications Act**, 18 U.S.C. § 2701–12 ("SCA"), provides special procedures for authorities to obtain such information without alerting the customer. In March 2018, the SCA was amended by the so-called **CLOUD Act** to include new procedures governing situations where data relating to personal communications are stored on servers outside the United States; these procedures generally permit US authorities to obtain such information if the service provider can access the data from within the United States, unless doing so might affect the privacy rights of a non-US citizen protected by the laws of a nation that has signed an appropriate agreement with the United States.

- *Metadata*. While data that constitute the content of communications have long been considered subject to the same protection as hard copies such as letters, the law has been less clear with respect to metadata, which typically do not reveal the content of what someone has communicated but rather other information connected with data communication storage or transmission. A recent decision of the Supreme Court held that to comply with the **Fourth Amendment**, prosecutors using the **Stored Communications Act** to obtain from cell phone service providers records showing the location of a customer must obtain a warrant supported by a showing of **probable cause**.

- *International cooperation*. A US prosecutor is increasingly able to obtain information—both documents and, if necessary, the testimony of witnesses—located outside of the territory of the United States, and the number of procedures available to do so and their efficacy have markedly increased over the last few years as national investigators have learned how to cooperate. To some degree, such cooperation may be informal; prosecutors (and regulators) increasingly tend to know each other, and at a minimum may take steps to simplify and accelerate formal means of cooperation. **Interpol** and other multinational agencies often coordinate contacts among investigators, especially with respect to international arrests. Different countries may set up **joint investigation forces** consisting of officers from more than one country working together on an investigation. Prosecutors also benefit from a variety of multilateral agreements, international treaties, and **mutual legal assistance treaties** ("MLATs") signed by two countries to coordinate exchanges of information, as well as relatively informal memoranda of understanding ("MOUs") signed by agencies in two countries. In some instances, a formal request for evidence from abroad will require the intervention of a judge.

Prior to trial, either the prosecutor or the defense can ask a court to "preserve" the testimony of a person whose presence cannot be assured at trial by obtaining a court-ordered **deposition** under Rule 15 of the Federal Rules of Criminal Procedure. For witnesses located outside the United States, a Rule 15 order is executed pursuant to the terms of the **Hague Convention on the Taking of Evidence Abroad in Civil or Commercial Matters**, or a similar multilateral or bilateral agreement, and pursuant to local procedures.

The United States is party to a number of bilateral and multilateral agreements concerning international **extradition**. Extradition—when the United States is either the "requesting" or the "requested" country—is largely handled under federal procedures. The basic provisions applicable to extradition proceedings when a foreign country requests extradition of a person found in the United States are found in 18 U.S.C. §§ 3182 et seq. In general, when responding to an extradition request from another country, the local **US Attorney** will appear in court seeking extradition on behalf of the foreign government.

D. USE OF THE GRAND JURY DURING AN INVESTIGATION

Review by grand jury BEFORE issuance of felony indictment

As noted in Chapter 6.B, review by a **grand jury** is required before the issuance of any felony **indictment** in federal and some state courts. At least in federal courts, the role of the grand jury in issuing an indictment is notably passive since its members rarely fail to authorize an indictment proposed by a prosecutor, but the institution of the grand jury (although not the individual members of it) is often nominally involved in obtaining evidence, especially from witnesses who refuse to be interviewed. While police officers and prosecutors cannot compel witnesses to submit to an interview (see Section B), the prosecutor may, in the name of the grand jury (but without any judicial review or approval or any act by the grand jury itself) issue a **subpoena** to a witness, compelling him to appear before the grand jury and testify **under oath** and on the record (i.e., with a verbatim **transcript**). Further, the prosecutor may in the name of a grand jury issue a **subpoena** *duces tecum*, which requires the recipient to produce to the grand jury documents or other information identified specifically or by category in the subpoena.

The procedures governing federal grand juries are addressed in Rule 6 of the Federal Rules of Criminal Procedure. Proceedings in the grand jury are secret and are *not* adversarial: the person against whom evidence is sought is not given notice of the issuance of a subpoena and has no ability to monitor, or seek judicial review of, its execution. A witness who receives a grand jury subpoena, who may or may not be a target of its investigation, may insist on a right not to incriminate himself, as set forth later in this section, and may also refuse to provide testimony or evidence that would violate a recognized privilege, such as the **attorney/client privilege**. In order to avoid a so-called perjury trap, where a prosecutor who already has abundant evidence of guilt induces the person involved to testify in the grand jury in order to develop an (often easily proved) **perjury** charge, a person subpoenaed to testify may ask if she is a **target** of the investigation. If the witness is a target—which is defined in Department of Justice **guidelines** as someone "as to whom the prose-cutor or the grand jury has substantial evidence linking him or her to the commission of a crime and who, in the judgment of the prosecutor, is a putative defendant"—she should be informed of this status. A recipient of an extremely overbroad subpoena *duces tecum* seeking documents may be tempted to seek judicial review of it by means of a **motion to quash** the subpoena. Such a motion is rarely granted other than in egregious cases, and in no event will such a motion provide a forum to ask a judge to review or supervise the grand jury investigation as a whole, nor can a subpoena recipient argue that the evidence sought is not relevant to the investigation. A more productive option is usually for a subpoena recipient to negotiate with the prosecutor a reduced scope of production.

A subpoenaed witness who fails without legal justification to answer questions or produce documents may be faced with a charge of **con-tempt**, which can be either a theoretically civil remedy or a criminal one. Civil contempt consists of an order by a judge that the person either pay a fine (often a recurring one, such as on a daily basis) or even stay in jail until she complies. Criminal contempt is in essence a stand-alone crime that could result in punishment by either a fine or imprisonment.

In order to protect the privacy of people or companies being investigated, Rule 6 of the Federal Rules of Criminal Procedure contains significant secrecy obligations applicable to the prosecutor and the grand jurors (as well as transcription typists and interpreters if one is present). Rule 6(e) contains specific provisions authorizing disclosures that a prosecutor may make of testimony or documents produced to the grand jury, which include disclosure of national security information to relevant authorities, and certain circumstances where disclosure can be made for other certain kinds of "judicial proceedings." A witness who appears before the grand jury, however, is under no obligation of secrecy, and is free to publicize the questions she was asked, although prosecutors often ask witnesses not to do this.

A person subpoenaed to appear before the grand jury who in good faith believes that an answer may tend to incriminate him may refuse to answer on that basis, relying on the **self-incrimination** clause of the **Fifth Amendment** of the Constitution. A corporation may not invoke the Fifth Amendment privilege against self-incrimination, and its officers must turn over information that may tend to incriminate the corporation or indeed other officers or employees of the corporation, although they could assert the privilege to avoid providing testimony that might incriminate themselves personally. If a prosecutor insists on hearing the evidence of an individual witness who "pleads the Fifth" and refuses to testify on this basis, she may invoke specific procedures to ask a judge to issue a so-called **immunity order,** which provides that neither the testimony given in the grand jury under the order nor evidence derived from it (known as "fruits") can be used as evidence against the witness. Thus, if a person testifies under immunity and is thereafter prosecuted, not only is the testimony given under the immunity order inadmissible as evidence against him, but the prosecutor must show that none of the evidence proffered at trial are "fruits" of the immunity order—that is, she must show that the trial evidence is "untainted" by the compelled testimony because it had an independent source. Since it is difficult, although not impossible, to convict someone who has testified under immunity, immunity orders are most often used to obtain information from "lower-downs" whom the prosecutor has no interest in prosecuting in order to obtain information about "higher-ups" in a gang or organization.

5 ARREST AND PRETRIAL DETENTION

A criminal matter becomes formally "adversarial" when a person who has been arrested and/or charged appears in court for the first time, since from that point on he will generally be represented by an attorney who will appear in court on his behalf. Such a first appearance is often caused by an **arraignment on an arrest**, as noted in Chapter 4. An arrest can occur either without an arrest warrant if the person responsible is caught *in flagrante* or if there is no time to obtain a warrant, or on the basis of a warrant issued by a judge. In the case of minor offenses, such as traffic violations, the police generally do not make an arrest; the alleged offender will instead receive an order, known as a **summons**, directing his appearance in court. A person who is indicted may agree to appear in court without having been arrested, often on the basis of an arrangement to do so with the prosecutor.

When an individual is arrested, he has a right to a prompt hearing before a judge to determine the terms upon which he may be released pending further proceedings. This first hearing, an **arraignment**, is also known as a **bail** hearing, and it must occur promptly after an arrest, generally within twenty-four hours. The prosecutor and a lawyer representing the person arrested (who is often assigned by the court if he lacks resources to hire an attorney) present their views on whether or not the defendant should be released and the conditions thereof. Traditionally, such conditions often require that an arrestee about whom there are concerns of flight "post bail"—a set amount of money (known as *cash bail*) that will be forfeited if he fails to reappear as ordered. In determining the conditions of release (and the amount of

[handwritten margin note: Arraignment, aka bail hearing]

41

bail if it is imposed), the judge must assess several factors, including the risk that the defendant will flee and not reappear, the links he has to the community, the possible danger of the individual to himself or the community, the seriousness of the offense, and the apparent strength of the case.

The cash bail system is increasingly criticized on the ground that it has a discriminatory impact on poor defendants. Many defendants are unable to post even modest amounts of bail. Some of them turn to **bail bondsmen,** who are entrepreneurs who will issue a "bond," an obligation to pay the amount of the bail if the defendant fails to show up. The terms of such bail bonds are often onerous, and many believe that the bail bondsmen—whose offices are often visible in the vicinity of courthouses, particularly in a big city—prey upon the vulnerable. People who are arrested and are unable to post cash bail simply remain in jail pending the outcome of their case. In a number of instances, those individuals may ultimately be offered a negotiated outcome, usually a **guilty plea,** that results in their being sentenced to **time served**—that is, their immediate release when the sentence consists of the time they have already spent in jail awaiting trial. Many commentators are concerned that this system—where a guilty plea is in essence an immediate means of escaping imprisonment for want of an ability to post bail—leads to guilty pleas where the defendant in fact has a meritorious defense but one that would take time to present at trial, pending which the person languishes in jail. A number of jurisdictions have abolished cash bail or are phasing it out. Alternatives to cash bail include frequent monitoring/reporting requirements, such as by electronic means, and a number of government and nongovernment organizations encourage the use of noncash alternatives to bail by providing services designed to ensure that an arrestee returns to court. Some defendants are released "on their own recognizance," meaning solely upon their promise—and a court order—that they will appear in court when necessary.

A person who fails to comply with orders to reappear in court upon release not only forfeits any cash bail that may have been posted, but commits a separate crime (known as **bail jumping**), and an **arrest warrant** will be issued for his arrest.

In the federal system, pursuant to Rule 5.1 of the F. R. Crim. P., a person who has been arrested or otherwise "charged with an offense other than a petty offense" has a right to a **preliminary hearing** at which the prosecutor must demonstrate that there is probable cause to believe that the defendant committed at least one of the crimes charged. Such a hearing amounts to a "mini-trial," at which the defendant has the right to cross-examine witnesses and introduce evidence. Preliminary hearings are, however, quite rare in the federal system, because the arrestee has no right to one once he is indicted. Prosecutors inevitably wish to avoid such a hearing and thus will generally arrange to obtain the indictment of an arrested individual within the time limits set forth in Rule 5.1—which provides that a hearing must take place "within a reasonable time," but no later than 14 days after arraignment if the defendant is in custody, or 21 days if the defendant has been released. Preliminary hearings are, however, common in some states.

6 THE DECISION TO PROSECUTE, OR NOT

A. PROSECUTORIAL DISCRETION

Prosecutors have virtually unfettered discretion over how to enforce the law, and in particular whether or not to prosecute a particular case. In the United States, there is no "principle of legality" that appears in the legal systems of some European and other countries providing that a prosecutor has a legal obligation to prosecute any case for which facts capable of proving guilt are present. As a result, many important decisions by a prosecutor are not reviewed by a judge or anyone else. This independence of the prosecutor—highly unusual by international standards (see Chapter 19)—is driven by the principle of **separation of powers**, which has been interpreted to mean that the **Constitution** allocates all such powers exclusively to the executive branch. Further, prosecutors are not held personally accountable for their prosecutorial decisions; they have virtually complete immunity from any legal challenge to their actions.

In any given case, a prosecutor can choose among a wide range of options: she may proceed with prosecution, usually by means of obtaining an **indictment**; she may decide not to prosecute and simply drop the case or stop investigating; or she may negotiate a consensual outcome, such as a **guilty plea** or a **deferred prosecution agreement**, as discussed in Chapter 11. The choice of which procedure to follow, and most of the steps in the execution of each, are entirely at the prosecutor's discretion.

A decision not to prosecute requires no documentation or explanation by the prosecutor at all, and cannot be reviewed by a judge, a person claiming to be a **victim** of the crime, or anyone else; there may not even be a formal record of it. Even once charges are filed, a prosecutor in the federal and most state systems has discretion to seek the **dismissal** of the case, and while the formal dismissal itself is made by a judge, he must follow a prosecutor's decision to do so in virtually all instances (see Chapter 11.B).

If a prosecutor elects to prosecute a person or corporation, for all crimes punishable by more than a year in prison (when applied to a person), in the federal and many state systems she must obtain the approval of the **grand jury** to obtain an **indictment** (see Chapter 6.B), but does not otherwise need to explain the decision; the prosecutor needs no judicial approval to charge a person with a crime, and an accused has virtually no opportunity to seek such review but rather must go to trial to defend against the accusation. In fact, individuals and companies have very limited procedural rights to be heard during an investigation at all. As set forth in Chapter 11.C and 11.D, judicial review of **negotiated outcomes** is limited to procedural requirements and, with respect to **guilty pleas**, to the appropriateness of the sentence. As noted in the Conclusion to this book, the practical effect of prosecutors' substantial and virtually unfettered control of many aspects of criminal justice in the United States has in the view of many, including this author, contributed to a fundamental imbalance of power and an erosion of constitutional protections.

[handwritten margin note: Normatively, should the review be substantive or well as procedural?]

[handwritten margin note: Too much power placed in prosecutors?]

Challenges to a prosecution based on a claim of "selective prosecution" are rare and difficult to sustain; to succeed in such a claim, an accused must demonstrate that prosecution in his specific case was driven by an impermissible motive, such as gender or race.

B. THE GRAND JURY

In the federal system, serious crimes cannot be prosecuted without the approval of a **grand jury**, a representative of which, along with the prosecutor, must sign an **indictment**. This requirement was adopted in the eighteenth century as a restraint on prosecutorial power, and in federal cases is required by the **Fifth Amendment**. Roughly half of the states follow the federal requirement of a grand jury, albeit often with different procedures. Thus a grand jury is a formalized step in felony prosecutions, but its role in overseeing prosecutorial discretion is limited as a practical matter.

A federal grand jury consists of twenty-three citizens randomly selected from voting records or other public lists. There are no qualifications to serve as a grand juror, and in fact, doing so is an obligation of any person summoned to serve. Sixteen grand jurors constitute a quorum, and twelve are necessary to approve a prosecutor's decision to prosecute. In a grand jury, a prosecutor interacts with the grand jurors, who are asked to hear evidence presented by the prosecutor and determine whether **probable cause** exists to conclude that the defendant committed the crime or crimes at issue. The prosecutor is virtually in total control of the grand jury proceedings; no judge is present. In the federal system, a grand jury proceeding is *not* adversarial; a person being investigated is not routinely given notice that matters pertaining to him are being heard by a grand jury and has no right to appear at it or contest its decision. The only persons present in addition to the witness are the prosecutor, the grand jurors, a stenographer, and (if necessary) an interpreter. The prosecutor has total control of the evidence submitted to the grand jury; she is under no formal obligation to produce **exculpatory evidence,** but need only introduce evidence sufficient to demonstrate probable cause that a crime was committed. The normal **rules of evidence**, such as the ban against **hearsay**, are inapplicable. Witnesses (including the person being investigated if called as a witness) testify **under oath**. They may not have an attorney present during the grand jury proceedings themselves, although they may consult with an attorney waiting outside the grand jury room. Grand jurors and prosecutors are under a strict obligation not to reveal or publicly discuss any aspect of grand jury proceedings unless so ordered by a judge or as part of subsequent criminal proceedings, although witnesses are under no such obligation. Leaks have been known to occur, but relatively infrequently.

In the federal system, and in most state systems as well, grand juries have little real impact on criminal justice because they are effectively controlled by the prosecutor; grand jurors themselves cannot initiate prosecutions or investigations, and do not frequently reject a prosecutor's request to indict. A few states authorize grand jurors to conduct certain investigations with greater freedom from the prosecutor.

"Indict a ham sandwich"

In the federal system, a decision by a prosecutor and a grand jury to indict an individual is not systematically reviewed by a judge, although in very limited (and relatively infrequent) instances, an accused may challenge the procedures by which the grand jurors were selected. If a defendant raises an objection to an indictment after trial, his challenge will likely be denied because any error in the indictment is considered per se harmless in light of the intervening **jury verdict** (*United States v. Mechanik*, 475 U.S. 66 [1986]). Some, but not all, states have adopted the rule of *Mechanik*.

In some states that require grand jury validation of an indictment, such as New York, a judge will—upon request by the defendant—review the transcript of the evidence before the grand jury to determine that it contains evidence showing probable cause that the defendant committed the crime or crimes of which he is accused.

In addition to having a role (albeit passive) in decisions regarding whether to indict, in the federal system, the grand jury is a principal means by which a prosecutor may compel testimony and order the production of documents, as set forth in Chapter 4.D.

C. THE INDICTMENT OR INFORMATION

The Federal Rules of Criminal Procedure require that an indictment "must be a plain, concise, and definite written statement of the essential facts constituting the offense charged," and must contain a specific reference to the criminal laws alleged to have been violated. The indictment thus recites facts that the prosecutor deems sufficient to convict the defendant if proven at trial. Although an indictment may in fact refer to specific evidence, it does not need to do so. There is also no requirement that the indictment recite *all* pertinent facts—only that the facts alleged are sufficient to satisfy the elements of the offense once proven. The **US Attorney** (or a member of her office) and the **foreperson** of the Grand Jury must sign the indictment.

For small crimes (known as **misdemeanors**) punishable by a term of imprisonment of one year or less, a federal prosecutor need not obtain an indictment from a grand jury but may proceed on the basis of an **information**, which looks just like an indictment but is signed only by the US Attorney or a staff member. Even in a felony case where grand jury approval is mandatory, a defendant may **waive** his right to have his case presented to a grand jury, in which case the prosecutor will use an information to charge the alleged offense; such a waiver of indictment often occurs in **negotiated outcomes** discussed in Chapter 11.

Some states do not have a grand jury requirement, allowing a prosecutor alone to initiate charges by filing an indictment. Several such states provide for a **preliminary hearing**, described in Chapter 5, as a means to ensure that the prosecutor has adequate grounds to indict.

7 JOINDER OF CHARGES AND DEFENDANTS

American criminal justice places a high value on judicial economy. As a result, the Federal Rules of Criminal Procedure permit prosecutors to join offenses and defendants in a single **indictment** or (where applicable) **information**, see Chapter 6.C. A case may thus proceed to trial with several defendants and may include several different charged offenses.

An indictment or information will typically list one or more **counts**, which are the specific charges against the defendants; each count must allege a specific, separate violation of one specific criminal law. Rule 8 of the Federal Rules of Criminal Procedure provides that an "indictment or information may charge a defendant in separate counts with two or more offenses if the offenses charged—whether felonies or misdemeanors or both—are of the same or similar character, or are based on the same act or transaction, or are connected with or constitute parts of a common scheme or plan." The indictment or information may also "charge two or more defendants if they are alleged to have participated in the same act or transaction, or in the same series of acts or transactions, constituting an offense or offenses. The defendants may be charged in one or more counts together or separately. All defendants need not be charged in each count."

The multiplication of counts may have an impact on **sentencing** because if a defendant is convicted, he may be separately sentenced on each count. And at sentencing, the judge may have discretion to impose **consecutive** or **concurrent** sentences, the former of which may significantly increase the maximum sentence (see Chapter 14).

49

Defendants often have concerns about being tried together, frequently fearing that the jury will use evidence against one defendant to infer the culpability of another, and may seek a **severance** in order to be tried separately. Judges infrequently grant severance, given their aim to promote judicial economy and consistent verdicts. The Supreme Court has stated that a severance is only appropriate where there is a serious risk that a joint trial would compromise a specific trial right of one defendant, or prevent the jury from making a reliable judgment about guilt or innocence (*Zafiro v. United States*, 560 U.S. 34 (1993)).

Joint trials can create so-called ***Bruton*** issues, after *Bruton v. United States*, 391 U.S. 123 (1969), when the prosecutor seeks to use as evidence a prior **confession** of one defendant that implicates another. If the confessing defendant does not testify at the joint trial, under *Bruton* and its progeny, his confession may be inadmissible against his codefendant, since it might deprive that codefendant of his constitutional right, under the **Confrontation Clause** of the **Sixth Amendment**, to confront adversarial witnesses in **cross-examination**. When faced with a request by one or more defendants to sever their trials from those of others because of a *Bruton* problem, a court will first explore whether it is possible to eliminate the conflict, perhaps by **redacting** the confession to eliminate reference to the non-confessing defendant. If this is insufficient (which may be the case if the statement clearly implicates a nonconfessing defendant, even if that person's name is removed), a court may order separate trials, although this does not happen frequently.

[handwritten margin note: Severance is granted only infrequently]

8 VENUE

Venue refers to the location of a criminal trial. In most cases, venue is noncontroversial, but in some instances it may be the subject of pretrial proceedings before a judge. Venue is in the first instance selected by the prosecutor, who (in a federal case) files charges in the district where the trial will take place. (As noted in Chapter 2.A.2, a **district** is an administrative subdivision of the federal courts, and some bigger states may have more than one federal district within their borders.) A defendant may seek a change of venue for several reasons.

The **Sixth Amendment** to the Constitution provides that a federal trial must occur in the state and district where a crime was committed. Venue must be proper for each **count** of an indictment or information. Defendants can waive venue either expressly or by failing to make a timely objection before trial. A defendant may move to transfer venue to another district in the same state on the grounds of prejudice if he can demonstrate that a trial in the venue selected by the prosecutor would be unfair, such as because publicity will affect the independence of jurors or because witnesses are otherwise unavailable.

While in most cases the location of the crime and thus the venue is obvious, complicated crimes may involve more than one district or state. A prosecutor's decision where to file charges may be reviewed by a court based on functional concerns, such as the convenience of the forum to the defendant and witnesses. Courts also aim to avoid gamesmanship known as "forum shopping" by defendants who may prefer to stand trial in one district over another.

9 ASSISTANCE OF COUNSEL

Participants in criminal justice systems have a constitutional right under the **Sixth Amendment** to "the assistance of counsel" at trial; the right to legal representation is also protected, and applicable to the states, by the Due Process Clause of the Fifth and Fourteenth Amendments. This right is zealously protected; failure to respect it may invalidate critical criminal procedures.

A. THE RIGHT TO COUNSEL

As a practical matter, the **right to counsel** may mean three similar and linked but nonetheless somewhat different things: (1) the right to insist that an attorney be present; (2) the right *to be informed* that one has a right to an attorney before proceeding; and (3) the right to have an attorney—whether privately retained or appointed to represent an indigent who cannot afford one—actually present before the case can proceed. With respect to (1), other than in the **grand jury** itself, any-one—even if not arrested or at apparent risk of being accused, such as a witness or even a victim—may wish to be accompanied by an attorney of her choice for advice or support, and generally has a right to do so in that the police or investigator cannot ask that the attorney be excluded. (Even in a grand jury proceeding, a witness may choose to have the advice of an attorney, even though that attorney must wait outside the grand jury room; see Chapter 3.D.) If not under arrest or at risk of accusation, a witness must on her own ask for an attorney and retain one herself, but in noncustodial and nonthreatening situations there is no obligation of state authorities to advise her of the right to have an attorney present, or to pay for one.

Certain stages of the criminal process, however, cannot proceed at all unless a person at risk is first informed of a right to counsel and is informed of a right to have counsel appointed at state expense if the person cannot afford one, and the process cannot continue unless the defendant affirmatively **waives** that right. As described in Chapter 4.B, under the Supreme Court's *Miranda v. Arizona* decision, a person whose liberty is constrained cannot be interrogated unless informed of his right to counsel (and to be informed of his right to silence and to be told any statements will be used against him). The right to be so informed at an interrogation does not lead to the immediate appointment of counsel for an indigent or even immediate access to an attorney personally retained, but rather should lead to the end of the interrogation, unless an appropriately informed person expressly waives that right (see Chapter 4.B).

In the third situation, when a defendant makes his first appearance in court, usually at an **arraignment** upon **arrest** or **indictment**, a person must not only be informed of the right to counsel before proceeding to the next step in the process, but counsel for those unable to afford one must actually be provided to appear in court on behalf of the accused, and no proceedings will take place until this is done.

Beyond constitutional guarantees where they apply, the practical necessity of counsel is difficult to overstate. Given the complexity of the law, procedures, and courts, defendants without experience struggle to navigate the justice system on their own.

A person with funds to pay for an attorney may choose and retain an attorney of his choice, subject only to the requirement that she be admitted to practice in the state where the trial takes place, as set forth in Chapter 18. In relatively unusual circumstances, a prosecutor may challenge a defendant's choice of attorney if the prosecutor feels that the attorney is subject to a conflict of interest, such as may occur if an attorney represents more than one person involved in an investigation (see Chapter 18.B on **conflicts of interest**). Attorneys are sometimes dismissed from a case if their schedule is too busy to permit the completion of proceedings on an appropriate schedule.

A person with inadequate funds has the right to an attorney compensated by the state at all stages from arrest or indictment through a trial and a direct appeal; the right to appointed counsel at later proceedings is less clear.

There are two approaches to providing state-compensated counsel. Individual attorneys licensed to practice law in that state (see Chapter 18. A) can apply to be on a list of attorneys who may be asked by the courts to represent indigent defendants, and are paid at a prescribed rate; some attorneys earn their living by obtaining such appointments. In federal cases, the practical procedures for compensating an attorney to represent indigent defendants are governed by the **Criminal Justice Act** ("CJA"), which is administered by the judges in each district. In addition, many jurisdictions create a law office—often called "Legal Aid" or "Public Defenders" or, in the federal system, "Federal Defenders"—to represent indigent defendants. The attorneys at such offices are paid a salary by the group by which they are employed, which in turn contracts with the relevant government (federal, state, or local) to represent individuals unable to hire their own attorney. An indigent defendant may not necessarily choose an attorney and then ask that the state compensate the attorney of his choice, but in most instances must accept the attorney (whether from the list of interested attorneys such as under the CJA, or from a Legal Aid/Federal Defenders office) appointed to represent him.

B. SELF-REPRESENTATION

The right to counsel includes the freedom to represent oneself and proceed without an attorney, which is known as proceeding *pro se* (*Faretta v. California*, 422 U.S. 806 (1975)). Of course, defendants who attempt to navigate the criminal justice system without an attorney to advise them may suffer as a result. A judge asked by a defendant to be permitted to proceed *pro se* must first obtain an express **waiver** from the defendant of his right to have an attorney, after giving extensive warnings—known as *Faretta* **warnings**—of the disadvantages and dangers of self-representation. A judge must also take steps to ensure that a defendant is competent to represent himself, and may refuse a defendant's choice to represent himself if he engages in serious misconduct to deliberately disrupt the trial. Judges sometimes appoint "shadow counsel" to be present in court on behalf of a defendant who has elected to represent himself and to offer advice even without speaking for the defendant.

C. INEFFECTIVE ASSISTANCE OF COUNSEL

The **right to counsel** implies not only that a criminal defendant has a right to an attorney to represent him at critical junctures of a criminal proceeding, but that that attorney's representation must meet at least minimum standards of professional responsibility. As noted in Chapter 18.B, an attorney's ethical and professional obligations include both a **duty of loyalty** (to avoid a **conflict of interest**, and to act solely in the client's interest) and a **duty of care**—that is, zealously to take all steps reasonably necessary to defend a client, such as pursuing legal defenses and locating evidence or witness testimony that may help establish a defense. A defendant who chooses (and pays for) his own attorney can of course replace that attorney, at least prior to trial, if unhappy with the attorney's efforts; once trial commences or is imminent, however, a judge may be unlikely to allow a defendant to replace his counsel. A defendant whose attorney has been appointed may be unhappy with that lawyer's efforts and seek to have him replaced, which a court may be unlikely to do absent fairly strong grounds to show that the attorney was unable to fulfill her responsibilities, although particularly at an early stage of representation a court may replace an appointed attorney—often at the attorney's request—if it is clear that the attorney and her client are unable to work together.

A defendant who is convicted sometimes blames the attorney, and may try to invalidate the conviction—either on appeal or post-conviction review, as set forth in Chapter 15—on the basis of claimed **ineffective assistance of counsel**. Because such claims risk undermining the finality of criminal convictions, and in particular may result in "second-guessing" of the trial lawyer's strategic decisions, the rules governing them are strict. As outlined by the Supreme Court in the case of *Strickland v. Washington*, 466 U.S. 668 (1984), to invalidate a conviction because of attorney incompetence, a defendant carries a heavy burden to show: (a) a clearly deficient performance, namely that the attorney's performance fell below any objective standard of reasonableness, and (b) prejudice, namely that it is reasonably probable that if the attorney had performed adequately, the result would have been different. Courts reviewing post-conviction ineffective assistance of counsel claims are particularly careful not to "second-guess" strategic decisions made by an attorney, even if the decisions turned out badly or seem ill-advised in retrospect. Many strategic questions are considered to fall within the ambit of professional competence, and an attorney's decision will not invalidate a conviction, even if the client disagreed with, or did not even know about, them. The conduct of oral presentations to a jury, whether and how to cross-examine, whether or not to object to the admission of evidence, whether and how to engage in motion practice— these and other decisions can be made by attorneys without consulting the client. A client must be consulted and approve of core decisions, which include whether or not to plead guilty (and the terms of any plea), whether or not to testify as a witness on his own behalf, and whether or not to appeal.

The constitutional right to effective assistance of counsel also applies to **plea negotiations**, discussed in Chapter 11.C. For example, a defense counsel's failure to inform her client of an advantageous plea offer may constitute a constitutional violation if the client goes to trial and receives a greater sentence than would have been imposed had the plea been accepted. The remedy for ineffective assistance of counsel at the plea negotiation stage may be the trial court's reissuing of the plea deal that had improperly been rejected, or the invalidation of a plea deal that had improperly been accepted. *Lafler v. Cooper*, 562 U.S. 1127 (2011). However, once again there is a strong presumption of attorney competence, and it is difficult to overturn a guilty plea or similar negotiated outcome based on a claim that the attorney's performance was deficient. Further, as noted in Chapter 11.C, the prosecutor may attempt to obtain a waiver of any right of a pleading defendant to appeal the plea.

10 TRIAL RIGHTS AND PREPARATION FOR TRIAL

A. THE RIGHT TO A SPEEDY TRIAL

The **Sixth Amendment** to the Constitution provides that an "accused shall enjoy the right to a speedy and public trial . . .." In federal courts, this right has been codified in the **Speedy Trial Act**, 18 U.S.C. § 3161–74, which requires that a trial begin within seventy days of the date of the filing of the **indictment** or **information** or of the date the defendant first appears in court, and has special provisions for a defendant in custody. The Act allows a judge to provide for longer periods only if based on a specific finding satisfying one or more permissible bases for delay listed in the Act. For example, the court may postpone trial for a period necessary to allow the parties to prepare for a complex case or while the judge is considering how to rule on motions made by the parties, or it may approve a longer period if the parties agree to an outcome such as a **deferred prosecution agreement,** as discussed in Chapter 11.D. However, the parties (prosecutor and defense) cannot simply agree among themselves to extend the time limits of the Act, but must persuade a judge that grounds exist to do so under one of the exceptions specifically permitted by the Act. This requirement not only protects defendants against agreements reached by prosecutors and defense attorneys to satisfy their own personal schedules, but also reflects the public's interest in a prompt trial.

Delays in an investigation where no indictment has been filed are generally addressed by the relevant **statute of limitations**. A defendant who claims that the indictment was filed after the expiration of the applicable statute of limitations must raise this issue prior to trial. The law on when the applicable period starts to run, and what events may either **toll** (or pause) its running, or satisfy it, is complex, and may vary among the various states and the federal government. The filing of an **indictment** or (where permitted) **information**—even if **sealed** and thus not public—generally stops the running of the applicable statute of limitations. In federal cases, the principal statute of limitations period is five years, 18 U.S.C. § 3282, although the legislation defining certain specific crimes provide for longer periods. The state statutes of limitations, as well as principles for their execution and interpretation, vary widely.

B. THE RIGHT OF ACCESS TO INFORMATION

Investigative and pretrial proceedings do not result in a formal "file" of the case in which one can expect to find all the evidence or other information relevant to it. While the court will maintain a **docket** for each case, which is open to the public (and often accessible electronically), the docket will only include the papers filed in court, and is not a repository for evidence as such. Rather, the prosecutor, working with the police, will compile the evidence she deems necessary to decide whether to charge a defendant and to support the prosecution's case at trial. Not all of this information will have been submitted to the **grand jury**, since the prosecutor need only introduce to the grand jury evidence sufficient to demonstrate probable cause that the defendant committed a crime; she does not need to submit all the evidence available to her. Neither the judge nor counsel for an accused has a systematic right of access to the entirety of the evidence or other information held by a prosecutor. Rather, in the federal system, defense access to such information is governed by several different provisions, known generally under the informal rubric of **discovery**. Inherent in these provisions is the essentially adversarial nature of the criminal process, since it involves one party (generally the defense) seeking information from an adversary (the prosecutor) who may be inclined to provide the minimum required by law. Counsel for a defendant must often be vigilant and proactive to make unambiguous requests for all the various kinds of possible information that a prosecutor may be required to share, absent which a failure of the prosecutor to share such information may be excused because of a **waiver** by the defendant.

Discovery procedure is one of the areas where there are often significant differences between federal and state regimes, and among the various states. In many instances, the federal procedures are less protective of the right of the defense to learn the evidence against the accused than is the case in some states.

The federal procedures include the following.

1. Rule 16

Rule 16 of the Federal Rules of Criminal Procedure requires the prosecution to disclose very specific information in response to a timely request from the defendant's attorney.

Information discoverable under Rule 16 includes written or recorded statements by the defendant, including the substance of oral statements if the prosecution intends to use them at trial, and documents and tangible objects that either belong to the defendant, will be offered by the prosecution at trial, or are material to preparing a defense. Rule 16 also requires disclosure of the defendant's criminal record, police reports, scientific reports, and expert witness testimony. There is, however, no formal requirement that the prosecutor share the names of all witnesses who may testify at trial, in part to avoid potential intimidation of witnesses.

2. 18 U.S.C. § 3500

If the prosecution calls a witness to testify at trial, Title 18, § 3500 of the United States Code and Rule 26.2 of the F. R. Crim. P. require that the prosecutor provide the defense with copies of all prior statements made by or attributed to the witness. This is often referred to as **Jencks material,** following a Supreme Court decision requiring such disclosure, *Jencks v. United States,* 353 U.S. 657 (1957). The purpose is to ensure that the defendant (and his lawyer) have access to any prior statements a witness has made, which are often the basis for

cross-examination at trial when (as is surprisingly often the case) a witness's trial testimony differs to some degree from prior statements. The formal requirement is that such material be shared with the defense only "[a]fter a witness ... has testified"—that is, during the trial itself—although in many instances prosecutors share such information earlier.

3. *Brady* and *Giglio* Material

Perhaps the most fundamental discovery obligations of a prosecutor are the result not of a written rule or a law, but derive from Supreme Court decisions interpreting the **Constitution**. Under the so-called *Brady* **rule**, named after the Supreme Court's decision in *Brady v. Maryland*, 373 U.S. 83 (1963), the prosecution has a general but very important obligation to disclose all evidence that is **exculpatory** to the defendant, or material to the defendant's guilt, and it must do so with sufficient time for the defense to investigate and use the evidence. This includes a duty not to produce false evidence (and to correct false evidence), as well as to share evidence tending to show the defendant's lack of responsibility, such as evidence showing that someone other than the defendant committed a crime for which the defendant is charged. Under the so-called *Giglio* **rule**, named after *Giglio v. United States*, 405 U.S. 150 (1972), the prosecutor must also share with the defense any evidence tending to show that a witness called by the prosecutor may lack credibility, such as evidence that the defense could use on cross-examination. Both *Brady* and *Giglio* rights must be vigorously asserted by the defense through unambiguous motions asking for such material, at risk of a finding (should pertinent evidence be discovered too late in a proceeding to be used at trial) that the defendant **waived** his rights.

Most prosecutors respect their obligations under these principles, and many engage in **open file discovery**—simply sharing everything they have—to avoid any misunderstanding. If it is discovered after a conviction that a prosecutor had failed to respect her obligations to provide *Brady* or *Giglio* evidence to the defense, even if inadvertently, the nondisclosure of significant information may be a ground to invalidate the conviction if it appears that the nondisclosed information would have had an impact on the outcome, had it been timely disclosed.

Collateral attacks of convictions, discussed in Chapter 15.G, are sometimes based on asserted violations of *Brady* and *Giglio* rights.

4. Discovery Rights of the Prosecutor

The Federal Rules of Criminal Procedure require the defense to produce certain documents, such as expert reports, expert witness testimony, and other records, but only if the defense itself requests production from the prosecution. The defense must also notify the prosecution of its intention to present specific defenses at trial, including an **alibi**, an **insanity defense**, and a defense that the alleged crime was committed in the exercise of public authority. If a defendant fails to comply with a specific pretrial discovery obligation, the court may disallow the defense or bar the defense from using evidence that should have been communicated to the prosecution. However, the defendant himself is under no obligation whatsoever to cooperate with the prosecution or the court in establishing the facts of the case; under no circumstances can the defendant be called upon—either before or during trial—to present evidence or explain facts other than as strictly set forth in Rule 16.

* * *

As noted in the Introduction and Conclusion of this book, leaving the crucial element of **discovery**—informing the defendant of the proof against him—to a process largely managed by adversaries is a distinctive, and potentially troubling, aspect of American criminal justice. Even though in the vast majority of cases the applicable procedures are followed appropriately and in good faith, the case law and literature reflect recurrent instances where prosecutors or police did not share exculpatory or mitigating evidence with an accused, which create worrisome doubts in the minds of some concerning how often such failures occur but are not detected.

The relative imbalance in access to information between the prosecution and the defense may be most extreme with respect to witness testimony. Unlike the professional rules in some countries, a prosecutor may meet with fact witnesses prior to trial to prepare them for trial testimony and generally does so, often at great length. They thereby have an intimate understanding not only of the detailed facts about which the witness may ultimately testify, but nuances in the witness's background, capacity to communicate, recollection of the events, and other parameters that may affect the credibility and weight of the ultimate testimony. Even when prosecutors fully and in good faith comply with Rule 16, the Jencks Act, the *Brady* and *Giglio* rules, and other discovery obligations, their understanding of key testimony is generally vastly greater than that of defense counsel, which allows them to craft their questions to witnesses with greater nuance, strategic precision, and confidence (among other reasons, because they generally can be sure they know the answer to any question they may ask of a witness whom they have "prepared"). This disparity is often accentuated because, at least in some jurisdictions, there is no formal obligation even to identify prosecution witnesses prior to calling them. While a few states, such as Florida, permit the defendant to learn of prospective witnesses' testimony against him by taking their oral depositions prior to trial, such procedures are rare.

The imbalance of access to information is critically important in plea negotiations. Some specific "discovery" rights (such as under 18 U.S.C. § 3500, discussed previously) can in principle only be enforced during a trial and even after a prosecution witness has testified. A defendant's right to discovery prior to or as a condition of plea negotiations is imprecise, and the subject of much debate. Further, as noted previously in the discussion of **pretrial detention**, a defendant unable to post **bail** and who thus remains in prison pending trial may be under intense pressure to reach a **negotiated outcome** that in some circumstances leads to his immediate release on a **time served** basis, which many defendants do. As a result, the most fundamental decision the defendant will make about his case is often reached at a time when the prosecutor may have much greater access to relevant information than does the pleading defendant.

C. OTHER PRETRIAL ACTIVITY

There is no way for a defendant to ask the court to decide the ultimate issue—whether or not the defendant is guilty—prior to trial. An energetic (and creative) lawyer may, however, attempt to limit the strength of the prosecutor's case by an array of applications (generally in the form of **motions**) filed with the judge before trial. As noted later, such motions often are part of a negotiating strategy whereby the defense attorney attempts to weaken the strength of the case against her client, and thereby induce a more favorable **negotiated outcome** (see Chapter 11.C.2). Such motions may include the following (in addition to **discovery** issues described in the previous section):

- *A motion to suppress.* The defendant may contest the **admissibility** of evidence that the prosecutor intends to use against him, often based on an argument that the evidence was illegally seized or was otherwise obtained in violation of the applicable laws including the Constitution, and thus subject to an **exclusionary rule**, as summarized in Chapters 4.B and 13.E. The judge may then hold an **evidentiary hearing** and hear testimony (for example, of police officers engaged in a challenged seizure). As a practical matter, the outcome of such a motion is often dispositive of the entire case, because many defendants elect to plead guilty if their efforts to suppress important evidence against them fail.
- *A motion directed to the indictment.* While in the federal system a judge cannot review an indictment as such to determine whether it was sufficiently supported by the facts, the defense counsel can sometimes argue in advance of trial that certain **counts** must be dismissed because they are based upon an inappropriate legal theory. Even if such a motion will not avoid a trial if even one count survives the motion, it may significantly decrease the defendant's sentencing exposure.
- *A motion in limine.* A defendant may anticipate that the prosecutor will present arguments to the jury that are legally inappropriate because they are based on a misreading of the law, or attempt to introduce certain evidence that does not satisfy the applicable **rules of evidence**. Such issues may sometimes be raised in advance of trial by a motion *in limine*, asking the court to exclude the argument or evidence.

Pretrial motions of this sort can be extremely important, even if they do not cause a dispositive result, because they can lead to an advantageous **negotiated outcome**: an experienced, thoughtful and assertive defense counsel can hope to diminish the strength of the prosecutor's case, and thereby be able to negotiate a better deal for her client.

In general, if the defendant has a legitimate complaint about any of the steps leading to trial—including anything relating to the investigation, the procedures before the grand jury, the form and content of the indictment, or venue—he must raise that complaint before trial, or else the issue will under most circumstances be deemed waived and thus not reviewable on appeal (see Chapter 15.C).

11 ALTERNATIVE OUTCOMES

In the United States, relatively few criminal matters go to trial. (Some of the possible reasons for this are summarized in the Conclusion; see Chapter 19.) Nationwide, more than 95 percent of criminal cases are resolved without a trial, and in the federal courts, the percentage is even higher. While many cases result in a **guilty plea**, there are other procedures that can also result in the termination of a criminal matter without a trial. Taken together, these procedures—in particular the power they give to prosecutors, and the relative absence of judicial participation or control—are among the most distinctive (and, to some, the most troubling) aspects of American criminal justice.

A. DIVERSION

A number of individual federal and state courts have developed innovative programs designed to cut down the enormous prison population of the United States, and to avoid where possible the sometimes brutal impact of prison on individuals and their families. While such **diversion programs** can take many forms, most consist of a screening mechanism to identify individuals who would be ineligible for such treatment—because of recidivism, the seriousness of their offense, or their apparent likelihood of violence, for example—followed by an agreed-upon period when the individual is required to participate in rehabilitation or education programs and to submit to monitoring or supervision, often under the auspices of a social services agency or a non-governmental organization (NGO). Such programs are developed by prosecutors' offices together with court administrative personnel, local bar groups, and participating NGOs. An agreement between a prosecutor and a defendant (and his attorney) to engage in such a diversion program will be presented to a judge, and is generally accepted. If the defendant satisfies the agreed-upon requirements and stays out of trouble, at the end of the relevant period, the case will be dismissed without the entry of a criminal conviction. While such programs were conceived to help individuals—often but not always young people and first offenders—these procedures have somewhat oddly evolved into **deferred prosecution agreements** (DPAs) and **non-prosecution agreements** (NPAs) available to large corporations, discussed in Section D.

B. DISMISSAL

Although the "pre-trial" period—after the filing of an **indictment** and prior to trial—is surprisingly free of formal procedural requirements, counsel for a defendant can and often do meet informally with prosecutors. In some circumstances, counsel can convince the prosecutor that the indictment was unfounded or should not be pursued for other reasons, and thus that the indictment should be dismissed. Sometimes a prosecutor will reach such a conclusion on her own, such as upon discovering an unanticipated weakness in the case. Once a prosecutor decides to dismiss an indictment, she can do so quite easily. In the federal system, Rule 48(a) of the F. R. Crim. P. provides that, prior to trial, a prosecutor may dismiss an indictment. While the rule conditions such a dismissal on "the leave [thus, permission] of the court," dismissals are generally considered to be entirely left to the discretion of the prosecutor; a judge cannot withhold permission to dismiss because he disagrees with the prosecutor's basis for doing so. Once trial commences, a dismissal can only be made with the consent of the defendant; this is because at that point the defendant may be protected by the principle of **double jeopardy** (see Chapter 12) and will want to be heard on the issue of whether the dismissal will permit a further prosecution. A dismissal may be either **with prejudice**, meaning that the prosecutor may not further prosecute the defendant for the same offense, or "without prejudice," in which case the indictment is dismissed but may be renewed. It is generally considered that a Rule 48 dismissal prior to trial is without prejudice unless the prosecutor specifies otherwise; if she specifies that the dismissal is with prejudice, then the dismissal has essentially the same preclusive effect as an **acquittal** because it bars subsequent prosecution for the same acts under the principle of **double jeopardy**, discussed in Chapter 12. Prosecutors need not give any reason for a decision to dismiss, although sometimes they do.

The **Department of Justice** (DOJ) has developed the similar concept of a **declination**, which refers to a decision not to prosecute a person (or, often, a corporation) under investigation who has not been indicted. Traditionally such decisions were neither formal nor public. More recently, however, the DOJ has stated that in certain areas it will publicly disseminate and explain the conditions necessary to convince prosecutors not to proceed against a person or entity—such as where the corporation **self-reports** an incident before it is discovered, and takes appropriate steps to avoid repetition—and that to encourage corporations to embrace self-regulation of this sort, it now sometimes publicizes the basis for a declination in an effort to provide guidance on corporate **compliance**.

C. GUILTY PLEAS

1. The Procedures

A **guilty plea** is a procedure by which a defendant admits guilt and a **judgment** of conviction is entered against him. F. R. Crim. P. 11 (**Rule 11**), which governs the procedures for guilty pleas in federal courts, also provides for a plea called *nolo contendere*, by which a judgment of conviction is entered against a defendant after he has agreed "not to contest" the allegations in an indictment. It differs from a guilty plea because in the absence of an admission of guilt, it may have fewer collateral consequences on the defendant in certain circumstances, such as a separate civil litigation. Unlike a guilty plea, a plea of *nolo contendere* can only be entered if the court has considered its impact on "the public interest in the administration of justice." *Nolo contendere* — rare pleas are disfavored and rarely used.

The guilty plea provisions of Rule 11 are quite detailed and provide a very specific procedural roadmap for guilty pleas, which judges must rigorously follow to avoid any possible attempt to revoke a plea later. The procedures are invoked only when the prosecutor and the defendant have agreed on the terms of the plea, which is included in a **plea agreement**. Such an agreement may be oral (and then set forth in detail in a transcript during the guilty plea proceeding) or in writing. Most complicated cases are resolved through a written plea agreement negotiated between the prosecutor and the defense, which are part of the public **docket**; they are often very detailed. In the federal system (some states differ), the court cannot be involved in plea discussions prior to the parties' reaching such an agreement, nor can a court order that they take place, although some judges manage to make known their view that plea negotiations would be a good idea.

judges not involved in guilty pleas, though sometimes influence subtly by way of suggestion

Overall, the guilty plea procedures that take place in court before a judge address two principal goals: to ensure that the defendant's plea is voluntary and is truly his decision, and to ensure that all elements of the "deal" are on the table, without any undisclosed promises.

To achieve the first goal, Rule 11(b) requires that the judge (who may put the defendant **under oath**, and often does) interrogate the defendant to make sure that he understands all the rights (to a trial by jury, to be able to cross examine witnesses against him, etc.) that he **waives** by entering a guilty plea, that the plea is voluntary and not based upon any threats or any promises other than those set forth in the plea agreement itself, and that there is a "factual basis for the plea." The court often satisfies the last element by interrogating the defendant: the judge will ask the defendant to state what he did to assure that the defendant has admitted facts that constitute the crime to which he is pleading guilty. The court will also generally ask the prosecutor to summarize the factual basis for the prosecution. It is important to emphasize, however, that the judge does not engage in any fact-finding other than hearing what the parties present to him, and thus there is no neutral evaluation of the case to determine its

Do judges ever find that there is an absence of factual basis?

factual basis. Although not specified in Rule 11, the court will also often query the defendant to ensure that he is not under any physical handicap, including the influence of drugs, when entering the plea, and that he has had an ample opportunity to consult with his attorney.

Rule 11(c), entitled "plea agreement procedure," sets forth the procedures to determine exactly what "deal" has been reached by the prosecution and the defendant. Ultimately, while the parties can negotiate and agree on a number of different issues (discussed later), by far the most important negotiation relates to the sentence that the judge will impose on the defendant. It is important to emphasize, however, that while the parties can agree on many points that bear on the sentence, in federal courts (many state procedures differ on this important point) in theory the parties cannot impose their views (or the terms of their agreement) on a judge to obtain a specific sentence, and the ultimate determination of the sentence at all times remains up to the judge, who, depending on the procedure used, imposes the sentence that he believes is most appropriate, or alternatively retains the right to disapprove the sentence to which the parties have agreed if he does not think it is appropriate. (The phenomenon of **mandatory minimum sentences** and their manipulation by prosecutors in the charging phase, which diminishes the control of judges over sentencing, will be discussed later in this section and in Chapter 14.B as well as in the Conclusion, Chapter 19.)

The most frequently used procedure, found in Rule 11(c)(1)(B), is that the prosecutor will agree to "recommend [to the judge], or agree not to oppose the defendant's request" for a specific sentence, that a particular range of sentences will be imposed, or that particular factors will apply to the sentence. The Rule specifies, however, that such a recommendation "does not bind the court." Thus, if a defendant pleads guilty under this provision, he will have the assurance of knowing the prosecutor's position on sentencing, but has no assurance what sentence the judge will actually impose, since the judge remains free to impose a different sentence, or to disregard the factors to which the prosecutor has agreed. In practice, the views expressed by the prosecutor carry such weight (see Chapter 14.C) that guilty pleas under this procedure are often attractive and lead to predicted outcomes, although in theory a defendant could be—and occasionally is—surprised if the judge finds the sentence to which a prosecutor has agreed is insufficient, because by then it is too late for the defendant to withdraw his plea on that basis.

Less frequently used is Rule 11(c)(1)(C), pursuant to which the parties agree not just to what position the prosecutor will recommend to the court, but on a specific sentence or range of sentences. As the Rule notes, this procedure "binds the court"—but only "once the court accepts the plea agreement," which the judge is free to reject if he finds the agreed-upon sentence inappropriate. It thus allows the judge to disapprove the entire proposed plea agreement, in which case the plea agreement is vacated, and the parties either renegotiate or go to trial. In practice, many judges faced with a Rule 11(c)(1)(C) plea agreement defer accepting or rejecting it until they receive the **presentencing report** that normally provides the basis for the determination of sentence (see Chapter 14.A) and only then make a decision whether or not to accept the plea.

If a judge fails to accept a plea for any reason, or if it is later withdrawn, the specific terms of Rule 410 of the **Federal Rules of Evidence** (as well as strong common law precedent designed to encourage guilty pleas) preclude the prosecutor from using anything said by or on behalf of the defendant, either in court or "during plea discussions," as proof against him at trial (although his plea statements can still be used to cross-examine him if he testifies and contradicts his plea allocution).

Key to plea negotiations is an agreement as to the **counts** to which a defendant pleads, since the prosecutor may agree to accept a guilty plea on lesser charges and then to **dismiss** other, more severe ones. In practice, this sometimes gives prosecutors immense power over sentences because certain charges may include **mandatory minimum sentences** that will be binding on the court if the defendant pleads guilty to it. For example, a prosecutor may insist on a plea to a charge that carries a mandatory minimum of five (or more) years, or alternatively to a plea to a lesser offense with no minimum. In either case, under Rule 11(c)(1)(B) the court may still have power to impose any sentence permitted by the guidelines above the mandatory minimum, but since in many instances the mandatory minimum is relatively high (and the judge has virtually no power to sentence more leniently), the risk that a defendant may face a mandatory minimum if convicted gives significant bargaining leverage to the prosecutor, since she can put immense pressure on a defendant to plead guilty to eliminate that risk.

The parties can also agree to other issues not directly related to the sentence.

- While appeals of guilty pleas are not generally fruitful, the plea agreement can (and often does) include an explicit waiver of a right to appeal.
- Alternatively, under Rule 11(a)(2), a defendant can enter into a so-called **conditional plea**, whereby he pleads guilty but is permitted to appeal an "adverse determination of a specified pretrial motion." These are discussed in the section on **appeals** in Chapter 16(B).
- Many agreements include an obligation by the defendant to **cooperate** with the prosecution by providing evidence against others, often including by testifying in court (see Chapter 14.C). Cooperation obligations inevitably obligate the defendant to provide "truthful" testimony, but are also inevitably one-sided in that they leave a determination of whether the cooperation was sufficient and truthful up to the prosecutor. When a defendant pleads guilty with a cooperation agreement that includes testifying in court against an accomplice, the prosecutor will often ask that sentencing of the pleading defendant be deferred until after the testimony.
- With the approval of the judge, the parties can agree to a provision for restitution to or reimbursement of **victims**.
- The parties can also agree to certain secondary (but nonetheless important) issues, such as whether the prosecution will seek the immediate incarceration of the defendant after a plea (if he is not already in custody pending trial), whether seized evidence will be returned to him, and other matters.

2. The Negotiations

The most important component of plea negotiations, of course, is also the most difficult to describe, which is how negotiations are conducted between the prosecutor and a defense attorney. Such discussions are private and informal, and do not take place in front of a judge; nor are such negotiations formally reported to a judge, although particularly in some state courts, judges often urge the parties to negotiate and ask to be kept informed.

Each negotiation is different. In very small cases, most often prosecuted in state rather than federal courts, the plea negotiations may be very rapid indeed. In fact, it is instructive to sit in big city criminal courts to see such pleas, which often appear to be (and in some instances are) quickly reached on almost an assembly-line basis because each case fits into parameters known to all the participants. In many small cases, a trial probably would not accomplish much if the proof, particularly based on an *in flagrante* arrest, is overwhelming; further, in some repetitive cases, the likely sentence is often not much of a mystery and can be quickly agreed upon.

Negotiations in larger and more complex cases can involve a wide variety of components and will resort to strategy, including bluffing. They constitute, in fact, a unique and sophisticated form of advocacy. A few elements are important.

- There is absolutely no professional inhibition on participating in, or even initiating, a plea negotiation. Such negotiations often begin at the suggestion of the defendant's counsel, but that is not always the case. In many cases, it might be considered inappropriate for defense counsel *not* to engage in some discussion with the prosecutor to explore the range of possible outcomes—and possibly in doing so to obtain some intelligence about how the prosecutor intends to try the case. Such a discussion might begin with an effort to persuade the prosecutor to **dismiss** or **decline** the case, as noted in section B, or to consider a **diversion program**, as noted in section A, and then turn to true negotiation if it credibly appears that the prosecutor has a strong case.

- It is important to note, as summarized in Chapter 18, that prosecutors and defense lawyers share the same profession, have had exactly the same legal training, and not infrequently either have had or will in the future have the position now occupied by their adversary. Such discussions are often fairly informal for this reason. Indeed, the adversaries often know each other, and at least may know the other's reputation for credibility and straightforwardness.

- As noted, Rule 410 of the **Federal Rules of Evidence** in federal cases, and well-known analogues in state cases, unambiguously protect the confidentiality of plea discussions (as well as the pleas themselves in the event that they are not accepted) against use at trial. A defendant and his counsel thus have a formal protection that the prosecutor cannot use anything said in discussions as evidence, which is designed to encourage such discussions. That said, of course, from the perspective of defense counsel, divulging any facts known to the defense – even if the defense statement itself cannot be used as evidence – nonetheless involving sharing information otherwise protected by the **attorney/client privilege** as discussed in Chapter 18(B), and may be of strategic value to the prosecutor. That does not at all mean that defense counsel cannot, or should not, share such information, only that doing so must be done carefully and with a strategic goal—and with the consent of the client.

- To ensure this confidentiality, the parties often engage in formal or informal agreements. A defense counsel may make what is known as a **proffer**, which is a description of what her client will testify if called upon to do so. This is particularly useful in cases where the prosecutor is considering an agreement based upon **cooperation**, since she can make a concrete proposal for a plea based on the proffer after evaluating how much value the cooperation will provide. A proffer is sometimes expressed, at least in the first instance, in hypothetical terms. If the parties agree to an interview between the prosecutor and the defendant himself, the interview is sometimes held under so-called **queen for a day** agreements, which reiterate that anything said by the defendant will not be used against him. An interview is not, however, without some strategic cost, since if plea negotiations fail and a case goes to trial, the prosecutor can use a defendant's statements (much like failed plea allocutions in court) to **impeach** a defendant who later testifies differently, and at a minimum the prosecutor will have a better understanding of the defendant's case and thus can adjust her strategy accordingly.

- It is important to understand the ethical and professional obligations of the defendant's lawyer in plea negotiations. Neither the defendant nor his attorney ever has an obligation to provide information to the prosecutor. But once an attorney enters into such negotiations, she must be straightforward. As a matter of professional ethics, a defense attorney has a **duty of candor** such that she cannot lie to a prosecutor, in negotiations or otherwise (see Chapter 18.B). And wholly apart from ethical considerations, lying to a prosecutor would generally be counterproductive since it is often very likely to be discovered, and once discovered would destroy the lawyer's credibility and greatly diminish the possibility of obtaining the best possible deal for a client.

- Strategically, a prosecutor considering a plea agreement, particularly if she is evaluating a possible **cooperation** agreement, generally wants to learn *everything* involved in a case, and not simply "the best case for the defense" that an attorney may advocate at trial, or a selective version of relevant events. If badly managed, this situation may cause an ethical dilemma for a defense attorney if she is asked to divulge information that may be hurtful to the client once known by the prosecutor. The key is that a defense lawyer unambiguously cannot share with a prosecutor information learned for a client—doing so would violate the **attorney/ client privilege** among other obligations—*unless* she and her client have decided that the best strategy is in at least exploring a negotiated outcome *and* they are sufficiently confident about the possible outcome and the agreed-upon procedures (such as a "queen for a day" agreement) to go forward. But once that point is reached, it is inevitably counterproductive for the defense attorney or her client to refuse to answer searching questions from a prosecutor, or pretend ignorance, or to dissemble: in most cases, prosecutors are simply too experienced and well-informed (and often have access to a wider range of facts than does the defendant's attorney) to accept a partial, skewed, or false version of events; an attempt to proceed on the basis of one risks losing any chance of an advantageous outcome if the prosecutor concludes that her negotiating partner is not negotiating credibly and in good faith.

- From a defense perspective, perhaps the most important element in plea negotiations (particularly in a complicated case) is to obtain a detailed understanding of the facts, whether by means of an **internal investigation** as described in Chapter 17 or otherwise. If a defense attorney achieves a factual mastery of a case that is superior to that of the prosecutor, that can provide a huge edge in negotiation – but by like token, an ill-informed defense counsel may be at a clear disadvantage. Such mastery of the facts may in some cases be difficult, but in that case resorting to guesswork or prevarication in exchanges with a prosecutor will almost inevitably lead to negative results.

At least to some degree, during negotiations both sides are evaluating risk: for the defense, the risk of conviction at trial, and especially the sentence that might ensue; for the prosecution, the risk of an acquittal. Particularly for the defense, this risk is consequential, since in most instances the penalty imposed after a trial will be higher—often much higher—than a penalty obtainable through negotiation. The existence of a perceived (and near-automatic) "plea discount" in sentencing is troubling to many, since it implies that the justice system puts a high cost on the exercise of a constitutional right to go to trial. And as noted in the Conclusion, the powers allocated to a prosecutor give her virtually unfettered power to induce guilty pleas in situations where she can condition escape from an onerous **mandatory minimum sentence** on an agreement to plead guilty.

Many participants and observers share a widespread concern that guilty pleas have become a baseline norm of criminal justice in the United States, possibly in part because without them the system would founder for lack of resources. And in fact, from a busy prosecutor's perspective, an inducement to engage in a plea (in addition to whatever risk of acquittal an individual case may present) is the simple efficiency of resolving the case without a trial, the preparation and conduct of which can be time-and resource-consuming. (The Conclusion, Chapter 19, will revisit this issue.)

In most cases, the possibility or plea negotiations drives defense strategy. The goal of many **pretrial motions** is often to increase bargaining leverage, as explored in Chapter 10.C, by diminishing the strength of the prosecutor's case or the likely range of sentencing outcomes in the event of a conviction.

D. CORPORATE DEFERRED AND NON-PROSECUTION AGREEMENTS

As noted previously, many jurisdictions provide for **diversion programs** that are designed to permit qualifying individuals—often young or first offenders—to avoid a trial or guilty plea, and the nefarious effect of a conviction, by agreeing to supervised measures designed to "return them to society" (see Chapter 11.A). Over the last twenty years, this practice has evolved in the area of corporate crime to permit corporations, often very large ones, to agree to complex and sometimes very significant obligations, including the payment of very large fines, without a criminal conviction. As we will explore in Chapter 16 on **corporate criminal responsibility**, for a variety of technical reasons in the United States, it is uncommonly hard to defend a corporation accused of a crime. But avoiding a formal judgment of conviction inevitably is viewed as advantageous to a corporation's reputation; some corporations also believe that a conviction amounts to a "corporate death penalty" if it would preclude them from being able to engage in certain kinds of economic activity, such as the ability to bid on public contracts, which under some circumstances may be a near-automatic result of a conviction. Prosecutors may also conclude that insisting on a trial or a guilty plea may harm employees and others associated with a corporation (who may, for example, lose their jobs if the company can no longer engage in business, even though they had nothing to do with the criminal wrongdoing). The procedures discussed here are those available in federal courts; some states and some administrative agencies such as the Securities and Exchange Commission have developed analogous provisions.

The common element of a **deferred prosecution agreement** (DPA) and a **non-prosecution agreement** (NPA) between a prosecutor and a corporate defendant is that the latter will agree to make substantial specified payments (often calculated under the **Federal Sentencing Guidelines** discussed in Chapter 14.B), to engage in remedial activities such as enhanced **compliance** measures, often to submit to supervision by a court-appointed **monitor** to ensure that it in fact respects its undertakings, and to accept responsibility for an agreed-upon statement of the facts that, absent an agreement, would have been part of the case against the corporation at trial or the basis for a guilty plea. If the corporation satisfactorily performs its agreement for a period of (usually) three years, it will be assured that it will face no prosecution based on the facts in question. Such agreements do not apply to the corporation's officers, employees, or other agents, although they may reach separate, and sometimes simultaneous, agreements with a prosecutor. In fact, most DPAs and NPAs include a very strong **cooperation agreement**, whereby the corporation agrees to share evidence and information available to it that may be used to prosecute individuals.

The difference between a DPA and an NPA is that in the former, formal charges are filed with the court—usually in the form of an **information** (see Chapter 6.C) based on the corporate defendant's **waiver** of a right to a grand jury indictment—and are then **dismissed with prejudice,** at the request of the prosecutor under F. R. Crim. P. 48 as set out in Chapter 11.B, upon the expiration of the agreed-upon period if the prosecutor concludes that the corporation has respected its obligations. A dismissal with prejudice gives legal protection to the defendant under **double jeopardy** principles (see

Chapter 12). In an NPA, nothing is filed with a court at all; the NPA is simply a contract between the prosecutor and the corporate defendant that the prosecutor will not bring charges based on the agreed-upon facts if the corporation respects its contractual obligations for the agreed-upon period, and upon completion of an NDA the corporation is only protected by that contractual promise. While relatively infrequent, there have been instances where a corporation signed a DPA or NPA, during the term of which the prosecutor concluded that the corporation had violated the agreement (either by continuing inappropriate behavior or by having failed to disclose all pertinent behavior at the time of the agreement), which resulted in vacating the agreement and reopening the case against the agreement (or agreeing to extended, and more onerous, terms).

One aspect of both DPAs and NPAs is that they are virtually free of any judicial supervision or review. Since DPAs and NPAs are agreements between prosecutor and corporate defendants that set out the penalty the corporation will pay and the conditions to which it will submit, they effectively allow the prosecutor to agree to sentencing terms without obtaining any review by a court of the appropriateness of that sentence—which, as noted previously, would not be the case if the corporation pleaded guilty, since under either **Rule 11** (c)(1)(B) or (C), the parties cannot divest the sentencing court of the power to impose or approve the sentence. This powerlessness of judges in dealing with DPAs was not immediately clear, but has now been emphasized in court decisions. In the case of a DPA where an **information** is filed, the court has a **docket** for the matter, and under the terms of the **Speedy Trial Act** (discussed in Chapter 10.A), it must make a determination that the DPA fits within an exception to the Act permitting the extension of the time during which trial must start, absent which the information would soon need to be dismissed for want of a speedy trial. A few federal judges attempted to use the fact that a DPA creates a judicial docket, and in particular the requirement in the STA that an extension avoiding dismissal can only be obtained "with the leave of the court," as a basis for them to review the DPA and possibly reject it as not being in the public interest, or at least to impose judicial oversight and conditions. Two federal courts of appeals, however, have concluded that courts can have virtually no role in the merits of DPAs at all (and by definition have none in NPAs, since nothing is filed with the court). Under the principle of **separation of powers**, these appellate courts reasoned, the decision whether or not to prosecute depends entirely on the prosecutor, and thus it does not fall within the power of the courts to review conditions that are a product of prosecutorial discretion, including whether its exercise is in the public interest. As a result, DPAs and NPAs—unlike their rough counterparts in the UK and in France and other countries where they are under consideration—depend exclusively on the outcome of negotiations between the prosecutor and the corporate defendant.

Separation of powers

Protection of prosecutorial decision from judicial oversight

12 DOUBLE JEOPARDY

Double jeopardy is the principle—known in Europe as *ne bis in idem*—that a person (including a corporation) should not be prosecuted twice for the same crime. In the United States, the principle is enshrined in the **Fifth Amendment** to the Constitution, which provides that "nor shall any person be subject for the same offence to be twice put in jeopardy of life or limb."

Notwithstanding its constitutional basis, the principle is subject to two interpretations in the United States that limit its effect.

First, the principle has long been subject to the "single sovereign" rule, and offers no protection if two different sovereigns engage in parallel or successive prosecutions. Thus under the current state of the law, if a person is convicted or acquitted in one state, that outcome does not bar further prosecution in another state, or by the federal government (and vice versa). Since this obviously raises questions of fairness, the **Department of Justice** issued the so-called **Petite Policy**, formally known as "Dual and Successive Prosecution Policy," which provides that prosecution in a state will generally bar federal prosecution based on the same facts, absent unusual circumstances such as indications that the state result was affected by incompetence or fraud, or in cases where there is an especially important federal interest. The Petite Policy is not a legal rule that is "binding" on the federal government and cannot be asserted in court as a protection against multiple prosecutions, but multiple prosecutions for the same facts are in fact infrequent. Very surprisingly, the Supreme Court in 2018 agreed to consider a case which challenges the basis for the "one sovereign" rule, and thus it may be curtailed, or even eliminated, in a decision expected in 2019.

Because of the "one sovereign" principle, US prosecutors do not consider themselves bound by criminal outcomes in a foreign country and will insist that they are free to prosecute a person or corporation a second time even if he or it has been convicted or acquitted outside of the United States. In May 2018, the DOJ issued **guidelines** where it indicated very generally that in a case where a corporation or person has already been convicted in another country, it will give consideration to whether the outcome of the foreign prosecution was adequate, in which case the DOJ might consider not bringing a second prosecution even if it could; this position is generally similar to the Petite Policy and like it is not binding on the federal prosecutor.

Second, the double jeopardy principle applies only to the risk of a true criminal judgment, not to administratively imposed noncorporal punishments, even if they may have onerous impacts comparable to an actual conviction. (The distinction between criminal and **administrative proceedings** is discussed in Chapter 1.) For example, in the area of securities violations and certain kinds of activity prohibited by the **Foreign Corrupt Practices Act,** the federal regulator—the **Securities and Exchange Commission** (SEC)—may seek huge fines in addition to the criminal penalties sought by a federal prosecutor against the same defendant and for the same facts; even though the "sovereign" is the same the courts have held that as long as the regulatory or administrative sanction is not clearly identified as "penal," its imposition does not trigger the Double Jeopardy clause. Taken together with the "one sovereign" principle, this means that a corporation or other person may face four separate adversaries—a federal prosecutor, a federal regulator, a state prosecutor, and a state regulator—and be forced to pay significant penalties to each for the same acts.

In those areas where the Double Jeopardy Clause does apply, its impact is straightforward: a person previously convicted or acquitted by the same sovereign has a right not to be prosecuted again for the same offense. This right must be asserted prior to trial in a **pretrial motion.** If a court determines that there has been a prior conviction or acquittal and that the "offense" (as well as the sovereign) is the same, it must dismiss a second prosecution.

13 THE TRIAL

We now come to trials. As noted in Chapter 11 and again in the Conclusion, Chapter 19, criminal trials are becoming less and less frequent in American criminal justice, virtually replaced by guilty pleas and other negotiated outcomes. But it is nonetheless critically important to understand their dynamics, because virtually the entire architecture of American criminal procedures is designed on the assumption that a trial—and particularly a jury trial—will take place as the ultimate check on the adversarial procedures in effect, and thus those procedures cannot make sense without understanding the trials around which they were conceived and developed.

There is no provision for **trial** *in absentia*, a trial in which the defendant is not physically present and without a specific consent from him. In federal courts, Rule 43 provides that a defendant "must be present . . . at every trial stage, including jury impanelment and the return of a verdict." The Rule does provide that a defendant may be "voluntarily absent after the trial has begun." Some states provide in theory that a trial can begin without the presence of the defendant if he was personally informed of the trial date and fails to appear without an adequate explanation, but in practice few judges commence a trial without the presence of the defendant. A corporation need not send a representative to a trial. Individual defendants may lose the right to be present if they persist in "disruptive behavior" after a warning, in which case the court may order in extreme cases that they be removed from the courtroom (possibly to follow the proceedings on a video connection).

A. THE ROLE OF THE JUDGE

As we have seen, during an investigation a judge has no continuous or systematic role, and does not participate or review a prosecutor's decision to prosecute; he may be called upon by the prosecutor where a judicial order is required, such as a **wiretap order**, an **arrest warrant**, or a **search warrant**, but does not otherwise get involved in the investigation (see Chapter 3).

Once an **indictment** has been filed, the judge will supervise pretrial preparations and set a trial date. During this period, as noted, the parties may ask the judge to intervene on a variety of possible pretrial issues, often by filing pretrial **motions** (see Chapter 10.C). Even during this stage, however, the judge does not engage in a systematic or formal review of the case going to trial, and often does not know, for example, exactly what proof will be offered by the prosecutor.

Once a trial begins, the judge:

- Will supervise the selection of the members of the jury, as set forth in the next section.
- Is *not* called upon to determine the guilt of the defendant in any case where there is a jury; absent very unusual circumstances discussed below where there has been a complete absence of proof on a necessary element, a judge must allow a jury to decide whether the defendant is guilty or not guilty, even if the judge personally would reach a different conclusion. In fact, the judge must not in any way convey to the jury his own thoughts on the defendant's culpability, or on the weight of any of the evidence including the credibility of witnesses, all of which is solely for the jury to decide.
- Supervises the conduct of the trial on a neutral basis, and must be scrupulously independent of both the prosecutor and the defense. In an important sense, the judge sets a dignified and solemn "tone" for the trial.
- Rules on the **admissibility** of evidence, and on any other objections raised by a party during the trial. It is often said that a judge performs a "gatekeeper function."

Judges are critical to maintaining an appropriate atmosphere, and to ensuring that a trial moves along efficiently and without undue waste of time. The judge's most important role is to safeguard the defendant's right to a fair trial.

B. THE RIGHT TO TRIAL BY JURY

The **Sixth Amendment** provides criminal defendants in federal
courts with the right to a **jury trial** before an impartial jury drawn
from the local "State and district." In the federal courts, there must be
twelve jurors who deliberate on the outcome of the case (unless the
judge finds "good cause" to excuse a juror after deliberations have
commenced, in which case there may be eleven). Various states have
different rules; some may have as few as six jurors at least in some
instances, although most require twelve.

The right to a jury trial has some exceptions. For crimes that carry
a maximum sentence of six months or less, there is no right to a jury
unless the defendant can demonstrate the seriousness of the offense.
If the prosecutor consents, defendants may **waive** the right to trial by
jury and proceed to a trial—called a **bench trial**—in which the judge
alone determines whether or not the defendant is guilty. In a federal
bench trial, either the defendant or the prosecutor may require that the
court "state its specific findings of fact" supporting a verdict of guilty or
not guilty. F. R. Crim. P. 23(c). This is profoundly different from a jury
trial, where the jurors make no factual findings at all about the basis for
their verdict. Since most defendants prefer to have their case heard by
a jury, bench trials are relatively infrequent. In rare instances,
a defendant will ask for a bench trial but the prosecutor can nonetheless
insist on a jury.

In federal cases, juries are selected "at random from a fair cross
section of community" in the district (28 U.S.C. § 1861). State procedures may vary to some degree but are generally similar. The process
begins with a screening of the **venire**, a panel of prospective jurors,
typically chosen at random from voter or motor registration records.
The judge screens the venire for individuals who may be exempt from
their duty to serve, including those who suffer economic hardship, have
health or hearing problems, face unavoidable parenting obligations,
lack of proficiency in English, or have employment conflicts. Short-
term excuses such as employment or vacation conflicts will generally
result in the prospective juror being recalled later. All US citizens are
under a legal obligation to serve as jurors in the state and **district** where

they live, and even if they may ultimately be excused must respond to a summons to appear for jury duty. While previously many jurisdictions provided for exemptions for certain categories of people, now there are relatively few people who can claim exemption because of their status or employment; doctors, lawyers, even judges may be called as jurors. And employers are legally obligated to allow employees to serve. Jurors receive a very modest stipend for each day they serve as jurors.

To select the final jurors for a particular trial from the remaining members of the venire after initial screening, the judge (or, in some jurisdictions, the attorneys) may ask a series of questions in a process called *voir dire*. These questions are intended to assess whether jurors are capable of impartiality at trial, including ensuring the absence of **conflicts of interest**. Based on the responses to these questions, either party may ask the judge to dismiss a potential juror **for cause** on the basis that the juror may lack objectivity. For example, a defendant may ask that a prospective juror from a family where many members serve in law enforcement be excused on the ground that she might unfairly support the position of the prosecution. Separately, both the prosecution and the defense may exercise a specified number of so-called **peremptory challenges,** which allows parties to dismiss a potential juror without providing a reason. In federal **felony** cases, where the defendant is charged with a crime punishable by imprisonment of more than one year, the prosecutor has six peremptory challenges and the defendant has ten (F. R. Crim. P. 24). If there are multiple defendants in the same trial, the number of peremptory challenges is increased.

The jury selection process is noteworthy, in comparison with procedures in other countries that have juries at all, by the degree to which the adversarial process enters into it. In practice, the two sides—prosecution and defense—may attempt to guess by means of observable data (such as a prospective juror's apparent age, race, and gender) and other information learned during *voir dire* (such as a juror's home neighborhood, education, or employment) whether such a person is likely to sympathize with the prosecution or the defense, or more precisely with the "narrative" that each will present during trial. While such determinations are inherently subjective, there exists a substantial body of academic research (the validity of which is not universally accepted) that may inform the parties' counsel on exercising their peremptory challenges to try to exclude jurors who might be sympathetic to the adversary. Thus, while the law aims in theory to produce juries that reflect a "cross-section of the community," the parties in the selection process may use their peremptory challenges, and strategically make challenges "for cause," in an attempt to skew the jury as best they can to exclude jurors deemed potentially hostile to their case. There is considerable controversy about the exercise of peremptory challenges, and some commentators have urged their abolition.

In *Batson v. Kentucky*, the Supreme Court held that peremptory challenges cannot be based on race, gender, or similar classifications (476 U.S. 79 (1986)). If it appears that one party is exercising peremptory challenges with a disproportionate effect on one race or other category, the court may require that party to justify the choices made in exercising peremptory challenges, and may disqualify a challenge if it is not persuaded that the reason given is legitimate and not based upon an improper factor.

The practice for jury selection in the various states varies widely. In some states, the prosecutor and counsel for the defendant may ask questions of potential jurors in an effort to determine if they bear any bias one way or another.

Jury selection in those states (and the federal government) where the **death penalty** is possible is particularly sensitive, controversial, and consequential. During *voir dire*, prospective jurors may be questioned about their views on the death penalty, and those who are systematically opposed to it may be stricken **for cause** if they acknowledge that they would not be able to consider its possibility. As noted in Chapter 14.D, the imposition of the death penalty is one of the very few areas where jurors must participate in the sentencing process.

C. THE DEFENDANT'S RIGHT TO REMAIN SILENT

A defendant has an absolute right to testify on his own behalf at trial, and if he does so, he is considered a witness like any other: he is put **under oath** and is subject to **cross-examination** by the prosecutor. On the other hand, the **self-incrimination** provision of the **Fifth Amendment** to the Constitution (which states that "no person" can "be compelled in any criminal case to be a witness against himself") also provides an absolute right *not* to testify. To protect that right, neither the prosecutor nor the judge can summon a defendant to testify at trial or call upon him to comment on the evidence; nor can a prosecutor attempt to call attention to a defendant's choice not to testify or urge the jury to draw an inference of guilt from that choice. Indeed, a defendant may request that the judge inform the jury that the defendant's silence is not indicative of guilt.

D. PRESUMPTIONS AND BURDENS OF PROOF

All criminal defendants have a constitutional right to the **presumption of innocence**. The neutral fact finder, be it a jury or a judge, must approach the case with the firm commitment that a defendant is innocent until proven guilty on the basis of evidence admitted at trial, and on no other basis. The **indictment**, even though voted by a grand jury, has no evidentiary weight and has not established anything; it is a mere accusation made by the prosecutor that she has yet to prove. The prosecutor carries the **burden of proof**; to overcome this burden, the prosecutor must convince the jury that the evidence submitted at trial and, subject to contestation by the defense, is sufficient to establish guilt **beyond a reasonable doubt**. That burden never shifts; the defendant is never under any obligation to prove his innocence (although a defendant may under certain circumstances be obliged to prove his entitlement to certain so-called **affirmative defenses**, such as a lack of responsibility; the procedures of the various states often differ on this point).

As a result of these principles, once a jury is selected and the trial begins, the "slate is clean" in the sense that nothing at all has been established: The jurors at this point know absolutely nothing about the case. While the judge may have some understanding of the underlying facts, that understanding is neither systematic nor comprehensive, and in any event is essentially irrelevant since all that counts is what the jurors will learn during the trial.

The presumption of innocence is thus not only an important principle of criminal justice, but also may guide defense strategy. Because the defendant does not have to prove anything at all, in many cases his best strategy may be, in essence, to remain as little noticed as possible, and for his attorney to keep the jurors' focus on the prosecution and its evidence—and to hold the prosecution to the high standard of "beyond a reasonable doubt." In other words, in some (but certainly not all) cases the defense does not want to propose an alternative set of facts, but rather insists that the prosecutor's evidence does not hold up under the scrutiny of cross-examination. And it bears emphasis that the ultimate verdict the jurors are asked to give is not whether or not the defendant is "innocent," but only whether or not he has been proven guilty.

E. THE RULES OF EVIDENCE AND EXCLUSIONARY RULES

All trials are governed by **rules of evidence**, which are numerous and often complex. Originally, evidentiary rules were developed by the **common law**. These rules are prescriptive, in the sense that they purport to state the principles applicable to different kinds of evidence to determine whether they are "admissible" and will be used at trial; such rules differ from the essentially "free proof" approach taken in many other countries, where virtually all pertinent evidence is considered for whatever it may add to the fact finders' understanding of the facts. In 1974, the rules were largely codified for federal proceedings in the **Federal Rules of Evidence**, the understanding and mastery of which are fundamentally important to all participants in federal trials and some other proceedings. Each state may have its own rules of evidence, which may be generally similar to—or even based upon—the federal rules, but only if that state legislature had adopted them. Rules of evidence govern **admissibility**—that is, whether evidence offered by a party will be made part of the record that is presented to the jurors and can be considered in their deliberations. Evidence offered by either side that a court finds to be inadmissible in most cases remains unknown to the jurors. Sometimes evidence is heard by a jury and then determined to have been inadmissible, in which case the court will direct that they disregard that evidence and not consider it in their deliberations. Obviously such an order to disregard is not likely to be effective if the inadmissible evidence is strong (such as the fact that a defendant confessed), thus it is imperative that defense counsel be vigilant to object to contested evidence before the jurors hear it.

The starting point in determining admissibility is that evidence must be deemed **relevant** to be admissible—that is, it must tend to show that a fact that could have an impact on the jury's decision is either "more or less probable than it would have been without the evidence." While relevance appears to be logical and straightforward in principle, in fact the relevance of some evidence is often hotly contested, and often depends on context. Even relevant evidence, however, may be deemed inadmissible by the judge, and thus withheld from the record. In some instances, the judge must follow specific rules limiting the admissibility of relevant evidence, the most notorious of which is the rule against **hearsay**—the principle that a witness can only testify to what he perceived himself, and cannot simply repeat what another may have told him—and its many exceptions. But in other instances, the judge may have discretion whether to admit evidence or not; for example, a judge may exclude evidence offered by either side if it is found to be duplicative, likely to confuse the jury because of its complexity, or a waste of time.

Separately from rules of evidence, certain evidence must be excluded in order to protect constitutional rights—the so-called **exclusionary rules**. The Supreme Court and other courts have developed rules relating to several aspects of criminal investigations, particularly custodial interviews, arrests, and searches of a person or property; and to deter noncompliance with these rules, the courts have developed principles governing whether evidence taken in violation of the Constitution can be admitted at trial. The subject is complex, but in general evidence taken in violation of the Constitution or of procedures specifically required by statute (such as for obtaining a **wiretap order**) may be subject to a **motion to suppress**, usually made before trial, and excluded from the record (see Chapter 10.C). The imposition of exclusionary rules to defer police misconduct is sometimes attacked on an argument that it does not make sense (in the words of a famous judge) that "the criminal is to go free because the constable has blundered," but they nonetheless have broadly been applied as constitutionally necessary to protect important rights.

The judge's administration of the **rules of evidence**—the "gate-keeper function" that determines the evidence that the jury hears—is critical to a fair trial and is frequently reviewed on appeal (see Chapter 15.D).

F. STRUCTURE OF THE TRIAL

1. Opening Statement

After the selection of the jury, the judge will briefly give an overview of how the trial will proceed, and then the trial commences with the **opening statement** of the prosecutor on behalf of the government, followed by an opening statement by the attorney for the defense if the defendant so wishes, although the defendant is not under any obliga-tion to make an opening statement. Opening statements, which may last only a few minutes or as long as an hour or more in a complicated case, provide opportunities for the opposing lawyers to give an over-view of the case and of the evidence that will be presented. The opposing attorneys may, for example, refer to key facts and witnesses, building a road map for jurors, which is often critical in complex matters. The opening statement is one of the few opportu-nities for attorneys to address the jurors directly. As noted above, the defense strategy in an opening is often not to outline what the defense will prove – since the defendant is under no obligation to prove any-thing – but rather to start the process of creating doubt about the strength of the prosecution case.

2. Presentation of Evidence

After opening statements, the prosecution must present its **case-in-chief.**

The examination of witnesses occupies the bulk of the trial. Compared with trials in many other countries, the tradition is that virtually all evidence comes from the mouths of, or at least is introduced by, witnesses who appear in front of the jurors and are subject to cross-examination. This is in part because the American criminal justice system is based on a fervent belief in the ability of jurors to evaluate the credibility of people whom they hear and see testify. As a result, as noted in Chapter 15.D under **appeals**, it is uncommonly difficult after a conviction to obtain review by claiming that the jurors gave improper weight to a witness's testimony. A further corollary of the primacy of witness testimony is that jurors are empowered to give it very great weight if they find the witness credible; in many (but not all) jurisdictions, for example, a defendant can be convicted on the testimony of a single witness, even an **accomplice**. In many trials, of course, the most important proof may consist of documents or other non-oral evidence, but even in such cases the relevant evidence is generally introduced through the testimony of a witness, who may be needed to establish the authenticity of a document or another prerequisite to its **admissibility**, and often to explain its context or its relevance to the case.

In what is known as **direct examination**, the prosecutor first calls a witness to testify, and questions the witness to elicit relevant evidence for the jury. A prosecutor may not on direct-examination ask **leading questions**—generally, questions that can be answered simply with a "yes" agreeing with the factual predicate of the question—which effectively prompt the witness to deliver the anticipated answer. If a defense attorney believes that a question is improper – either in form, such as being a leading question, or because the question may lead to inadmissible evidence – she must immediately state an **objection**, which the judge will either accept ("sustain") or reject ("overrule"). If the issue raised by an objection is complicated, the judge may hear the opposing parties on their respective arguments, generally out of the hearing of the jury in a so-called **sidebar**. Counsel must be vigilant to spot improper questions or testimony; a failure to make a timely and appropriate objection may later mean that an appellate court will not review it (see Chapter 15.D). For example, some objections may be to the "form" of a question, which could be easily remedied in response to an objection. Witnesses unable to speak English testify with the aid of an interpreter, whose competence must be verified by the judge.

The defense then has the opportunity to ask each witness questions in **cross-examination**, which occurs immediately after direct examination. On cross-examination, the prohibition on leading questions does not apply. The goal of cross-examination is often to challenge statements that the witness made on direct examination by eliciting doubt about his knowledge, credibility, or capacity to recollect facts. The defense may try to **impeach** the witness by asking questions about the witness's own past, which may be permissible if those facts relate to the witness's credibility or bias. If a witness has made prior statements that are in the possession of the prosecution, under the **Jencks Act** such statements will have been provided to the defense (see Chapter 10.B.2) and witnesses are frequently cross-examined about any discrepancies that may appear in them. If there is more than one defendant, each may cross-examine a prosecution witness, although the trial judge may limit questions if they simply repeat questions already asked by another attorney. Cross-examination – which one leading and oft-quoted scholar described as "beyond any doubt the greatest legal engine ever invented for the discovery of truth" – is often the most important, as well as the most dramatic, element in a criminal trial.

Following cross-examination, the prosecutor then has a second opportunity to question the same witness, in **redirect examination**, often to restore the witness's credibility. On redirect examination, the prosecutor is limited to points raised on cross-examination, and she may not ask the witness to simply repeat his testimony. This back-and-forth questioning is at the heart of the adversarial process. When the parties have finished their respective examinations of a witness, he is excused by the court. In most instances, witnesses (other than a party) are not permitted in the courtroom to hear testimony of prior witnesses testifying in the same case.

Either the prosecution or the defense may call a witness and ask that the witness be qualified as an **expert**. Under Rules 701 *et seq.* of the **Federal Rules of Evidence** applicable in federal cases, the judge must determine if a proffered witness in fact has the "knowledge, skill, experience, training or education" that will "help the trier of fact [in criminal cases, generally the jurors] to understand the evidence or to determine a fact in issue." A witness qualified by the judge to speak as an expert can give an opinion, but an expert may not offer an opinion about the guilt or innocence of the accused. Expert witnesses are almost always chosen and retained by the prosecution or the defense; particularly in criminal jury cases, experts are not selected or questioned by the judge. Often both sides choose opposing experts on the same issue, creating what is sometimes known as a "battle of the experts." Some areas where experts often provide testimony are forensic matters such as finger-prints, DNA, ballistic tests of firearms, and chemical analysis of drugs; the mental state of the accused if a defense of insanity or diminished culpability is raised; and statistical analyses in complex financial cases. There is currently a vigorous debate about the admissibility of expert testimony on essentially psychological issues such as whether a confession was invo-luntary or whether an eye-witness identification was prone to error.

All witness testimony is transcribed verbatim by an official **court reporter**, and the **transcript** becomes part of the court **record**. Colloquy among the judge and attorneys for the parties, even if out of the presence of the jury, is generally transcribed, although the judge may direct that informal discussion be "off the record" (that is, not transcribed) and then summarized.

During the trial, either side may offer documents or physical objects as evidence during the course of the examination of a witness. The judge must rule on the **admissibility** of each document or item so offered, which must comply with the **rules of evidence** as previously discussed. Sometimes the prosecution and the defense will agree on the admissibility of a document or another piece of evidence, which is often expressed in a written **stipulation**, without the need for a witness. Once admitted, such pieces of evidence become part of the formal record of the trial as **exhibits**, along with the transcript of the witnesses' testi-mony. They are assigned sequential "exhibit numbers" for reference.

3. Trial Motions

Once the prosecutor has presented all of her witnesses, documents, and other evidence (and prosecution witnesses have been cross-examined), the prosecution "rests," indicating that it has completed presentation of proof on behalf of the prosecution. At this time, the defense may submit a **motion for a judgment of acquittal** of any or all of the charges, arguing that the prosecution has failed to produce evidence sufficient to meet its **burden of proof**. The judge may grant or deny the motion, or he may reserve the decision for a later time in the proceeding (F. R. Crim. P. 29).

It is essential to understand the role and very limited power of the judge in ruling on motions for a judgment of acquittal. In so ruling, the judge does *not* make a finding of whether or not the defendant is guilty, and in particular the judge never decides whether one or another witness was credible, since such issues are solely for the jury to decide. Rather, the judge can rule in favor of a defendant only if the judge finds that *even if* all issues of credibility are resolved in favor of the prosecution—or, as it is sometimes put, when the evidence is viewed "in the light most favorable to the prosecution"— no reasonable juror could find the defendant guilty. Sometimes, the prosecutor may simply have failed to introduce evidence of a required element of the offense, perhaps because of an incorrect understanding of the law, or perhaps through oversight or the unavailability of a witness or other proof. And in some instances, the court may conclude that the prosecution's case depends on inferences that are insufficiently rational. For example, in a narcotics case, a judge might conclude that the "mere presence" of the defendant near a place where others sold narcotics is insufficient to show that the defendant participated in the sale; on the other hand, even slight additional evidence—such as that the defendant acted in a way suggesting an awareness that his conduct was illegal, or that he was acting as a lookout—may be considered enough to allow the jury to decide the issue of culpability.

A judge may grant a motion with respect to any or all of the different **counts**. If the judge grants a motion for a judgment of acquittal, a judgment of "not guilty" is entered on the relevant count or counts, with the same force and effect as a jury verdict acquitting the defendant and the case is over (at least on that count)—that is, the prosecutor can neither appeal the judgment nor attempt to try the defendant on that count again. The only way in the federal system where a judge can, in essence, permit appellate review of a decision by a judge to acquit because of insufficient evidence is if the judge reserves a decision on a motion for a judgment of acquittal, permits the jury to decide the guilt or nonguilt of the defendant, and in the event of a guilty verdict *then* grants the motion for a judgment of acquittal. The prosecutor can appeal this ruling, and if she prevails, then the jury verdict will be reinstated.

Overall, however, grants of a motion for a judgment of acquittal are relatively infrequent, and appellate review of them under the procedure noted here is rare.

If the judge does not grant the motion, the defendant has an opportunity to present evidence in his defense, although a defendant is never under an obligation to introduce evidence, and often does not. The same process of direct and cross-examination ensues for defense witnesses, although now it is the defense counsel who cannot ask leading questions of a witness she has called. If the defendant elects to testify, he is under oath and is subject to cross-examination like any other witness. After the defense has rested, the government may present **rebuttal witnesses** or new evidence not included in its case-in-chief to address anything new raised in the defense case, but not to repeat evidence already presented in the case-in-chief. After both parties have submitted all of their evidence, the defense may again submit a motion for a judgment of acquittal.

4. Closing Statements

After the presentation of all evidence—that is, when both parties have "rested"—the prosecutor and counsel for the defendant deliver oral **closing arguments**, often called a **summation**. The advocates sometimes use visual aids to summarize evidence and help convey their argument. The prosecutor presents her closing argument first, followed by an attorney for the defense, and the prosecutor may respond to the defense in a short rebuttal. (Although traditionally defense counsel spoke last, in federal courts the rule was changed so that prosecutors speak last on the theory that it is the prosecutor who bears the burden of proof.) If there is more than one defendant, counsel for each may address the jury. Such arguments are the only opportunity, other than opening statements, for attorneys to address the jurors directly. Closing statements may be short, but in complex cases may be several hours long; the judge will indicate before they begin how much time he will permit for them. In their arguments, the opposing sides will argue why the evidence does, or does not, suffice to find the defendant guilty. During their arguments, the lawyers can only refer to evidence that has been admitted during the trial. Neither the prosecutor nor a defense lawyer can express a personal view about the guilt of the defendant, or offer a personal opinion about the credibility of a witness or the weight of evidence.

5. Jury Instructions

At this point, the judge delivers **jury instructions,** also known as the judge's **charge,** to the jury. Because the jurors deliberate alone and without participation by the judge and cannot be questioned about the basis for their verdict, the instructions are the only means by which the judge can be sure that the jurors understand the relevant laws and procedures that they must apply when they deliberate. Judges often tell jurors, "You are in charge of deciding the facts, but you must listen to me when I explain the law." Because of the sensitivity of jury instructions—which are often reviewed on appeal, as explained in Chapter 15.D—the judge will share with the parties the language he proposes to use, and the parties may submit their own suggestions. This is done in a conference, out of the presence of the jury, which takes place before closing arguments so that when delivering their summations, the attorneys know what language the court will use in describing the law to the jurors—and thus can attempt to tailor their comments to address the legal issues as the jurors will hear them. In a complex case, it may take an hour or more for the judge to read all of the instructions to the jury. The jury instructions will itemize each element that the jurors must find to have been proven in order to convict on each count, tell the jury how to proceed with their deliberations, and define principles such as the meaning of **beyond a reasonable doubt** and the requirement of **unanimity.**

"Model" jury instructions covering general criminal procedure principles and the elements for principal crimes are published applicable to federal and state matters, and judges often begin with such models and then edit them for appropriateness and applicability in a particular case. The judge does not summarize or refer to the evidence offered by either side, does not comment on the credibility of any witness, and in general must rigorously avoid saying anything that might appear to favor the prosecution or the defense, or how the judge views the facts.

At the request of either the prosecutor or a defendant, and in an appropriate context, the judge will also instruct the jury that they may convict a defendant of a **lesser included offense** in the event that they fail to reach agreement with respect to one of the elements of a charge against that defendant but do reach agreement on all of the other elements if the remaining elements themselves constitute a crime. The classic example of a lesser included offense is that a defendant may be accused of intentional homicide, which requires proof that the defendant specifically intended to kill. The jurors may find all the elements of the crime of homicide other than intent. In that event, rather than acquitting—which they would necessarily do if not given the option of convicting on a lesser included offense—they can convict on the crime of manslaughter (involuntary homicide), which shares all of the elements of intentional homicide other than intent. A number of crimes found in both federal and state laws contained lesser included crimes. An instruction permitting jurors to do this is appropriate only if the court finds that the lesser charge is, in the words of Rule 31(c) of the Federal Rules of Criminal Procedure, "necessarily included in the offense charged."

6. Jury Deliberations and Verdict

The jurors then deliberate by themselves in total secrecy. They are rigorously secluded from any contact with participants in the trial, and are admonished not to discuss the case with anyone, including their own family or friends, nor to engage in any inquiry by means of internet research on a cell phone or computer. In very infrequent circumstances where there is a risk that someone might attempt to influence the members of the jury, their names may not be publicly released, and they may be housed in a hotel during deliberations. They cannot confer with the judge; if the jurors have any questions during their deliberations, they will communicate each question in a written note to the judge. Such questions may ask for specific testimonial evidence to be read to them from the transcript, to see a document or object admitted into evidence, or to have a point of law (from the jury instructions) repeated for them. The judge will consult with the prosecutor and counsel for the defense before responding to the jurors' questions in open court.

Although the Constitution does not mention **unanimity**, federal courts require unanimous agreement on each element of an offense to enter a verdict of either guilty or not guilty on each count. Most but not all states also require unanimity in jury verdicts; the few that do not require a supermajority.

If the jurors reach a unanimous verdict, they will so inform the judge by a written note (or sometimes a **verdict form** that lists each count and where the jury can check "guilty" or "not guilty") and then will announce their verdict orally in open court. For each count, the verdict is either "guilty" or "not guilty"; the jurors do not make any finding as to whether a defendant is "innocent." In most circumstances they do not provide any explanation for their verdict; in some instances the judge may ask them to indicate on their jury form whether or not they have found each separate element of each offense, but this practice is discouraged, especially in the federal system, and rare. If either party requests, the judge may—and traditionally often does—**poll** the jurors individually, which means to ask each juror, on each count, what is his or her verdict; this is done to ensure unanimity. Once a verdict has been entered on each count, the jurors are dismissed. They are not under a legal obligation to keep their deliberations secret, and may be interviewed by the press or the parties, although jurors also have a right not to discuss their deliberations if they choose not to. If the verdict is guilty on any count, the judge will set a date for the imposition of the sentence, usually several weeks later. In some circumstances, the prosecution may ask that the judge "remand"—that is, put in custody—a convicted defendant on the ground that he now has an incentive to flee, but a judge has full discretion to allow a defendant not already in custody to remain free pending sentencing.

If the jurors are unable to reach a unanimous verdict on any **count** and so inform the judge by a written note, the judge will in the first instance often ask them to continue their deliberations to see if they can reach a verdict, a procedure known as an **Allen charge**, based on a decision permitting it. Once it becomes clear that no verdict is likely to be forthcoming because the jurors cannot reach a unanimous verdict on any count, the judge may order a **mistrial** of the entire case, which means that the trial ends without any finding of guilt or nonguilt. This is often referred to as a **hung jury**. If the jury reaches a unanimous verdict (of either guilty or not guilty) on some counts but "hangs" on others, a verdict can be entered on those counts where the jurors agreed, and a mistrial can be entered on the others. In other words, a failure to convict the defendant on a particular count because the jury lacked unanimity to do so does not result in an acquittal, which can occur only if the jurors are unanimous in saying that the defendant is "not guilty" on that count. After a partial or total mistrial, the prosecution may elect (but is not obligated) to try the defendant again on the unresolved counts, which will happen in a new trial before an entirely new jury, at which trial all of the evidence will be presented anew and all of the procedures summarized here repeated. At a second trial, nothing will have been established by the first trial: the members of a new jury will hear the evidence presented to them on the same basis as the first jury, and are not necessarily even aware that an earlier trial has taken place. There is no formal or legal limit to the number of "hung jury" mistrials that can be retried, but it is rare that a prosecutor will attempt more than three before abandoning the case. A prosecutor's decision whether or not to seek retrial of a defendant after a mistrial may be based in part on informally speaking with the jurors who were unable to reach unanimous agreement; a prosecutor would be more likely to seek a retrial if the first trial "hung" only because one or two jurors disagreed with the majority, but would be less likely to do so if a majority favored acquittal. Informal interviews with jurors may also inform the prosecutor about what evidence they found particularly persuasive, or unpersuasive, which may allow her to readjust her strategy accordingly in a retrial.

Mistrials can also occur, at the request of one of the parties or even on the judge's own initiative, when an unanticipated event either makes a jury verdict impossible (if, for example, so many jurors become ill that the minimum necessary for a quorum are no longer present) or if one or another party has rendered the trial improper or unfair through inappropriate conduct. Under some circumstances, especially if a mistrial occurs because of improper conduct by the prosecutor, the defendant may argue that a retrial should be barred because of the **double jeopardy** principle, but in most cases a mistrial does not preclude a new trial.

A defendant convicted by a jury cannot attempt to attack the verdict by speaking to jurors and then arguing to a court that the jurors' verdict was based on faulty reasoning. Rather, a jury verdict may be **impeached** only on one of two bases. If it appears that there was an outside influence on the jury (such as unauthorized contact with them, or where they conducted their own inquiries into the matter) and that the influence may have had an impact on the verdict, a judge may (after careful inquiry, which may include interviews with some or all of the jurors) order a new trial. And if the parties learn that the jury may have considered an inappropriate basis such as the race or ethnicity of the defendant, and it appears that this had an impact on the verdict, a judge may also order a new trial. Such actions are infrequent.

G. BEYOND A REASONABLE DOUBT STANDARD

Jurors are instructed that they can convict only if they are convinced of guilt **beyond a reasonable doubt. Jury instructions** on this point generally state that if a juror has "a doubt based on reason" after reviewing all of the evidence, he or she must vote "not guilty," even if the juror believes that the defendant is probably guilty. Jurors vote only "guilty" or "not guilty"; they are never asked to determine whether or not the defendant is "innocent," nor do they explain the basis for or the reasoning behind their verdict.

H. THE EFFECT OF AN ACQUITTAL

If a defendant is acquitted after trial, most often by a jury verdict but occasionally by a judge's decision as summarized in section F (3), the acquittal is filed as a formal **judgment**. That judgment may have preclusive effect on future prosecution under the principle barring **double jeopardy**, as discussed in Chapter 12. Since such a judgment only means that he was not found guilty beyond a reasonable doubt, it does not follow that an acquitted defendant can claim to have been "found innocent"—although of course many do. For this reason, an acquittal in a criminal case does not categorically preclude responsibility for civil damages for the same acts, including in a civil suit brought by a victim. An acquitted defendant is not systematically entitled to reimbursement of costs or attorneys' fees.

I. THE JURY'S ROLE IN SENTENCING

In most instances in federal court, the **sentence** is imposed, usually several weeks after the trial verdict, by the judge and without any participation by the jurors, who are not asked to consider sentencing during their deliberations (see Chapter 14). As set forth in Chapter 14. D, there are very limited situations in which a jury must address sentencing at all. If the statutory scheme permits a sentence beyond the statutory maximum in the event that certain facts have occurred (such as a particularly atrocious crime or a crime committed on a minor or disabled person), the jury must make the factual determination of the additional element required to impose the higher sentence; however, the fact of a prior conviction may be proved by a copy of the judgment alone. Similarly, any fact that increases the **mandatory minimum sentence** must be specifically determined by the jury, as part of their verdict. If the **death penalty** is applicable and is sought by the prosecutor, the jury must find that the facts suffice to impose a sentence of death. Chapter 14.D

J. THE PUBLIC'S AND VICTIM'S RIGHTS

A defendant in federal court has a right under the **Sixth Amendment** of the Constitution to a "speedy and *public* trial." The **First Amendment** also protects the public's right to observe trials and of the press to cover them. Both provisions reflect a deep commitment that proceedings relating to criminal justice, especially trials, be open and transparent.

The court's priority is to ensure that defendants receive fair trials, which sometimes may conflict with the rights of parties to speak publicly. It is often said that criminal matters should be litigated in court and not "in the court of public opinion," and attorneys who are professionally involved in a criminal case are ethically constrained not to make public statements "that might reasonably be expected" to have an impact on it, particularly in anticipation of or during a jury trial. In very unusual circumstances of misconduct, a court may issue a **gag order**, prohibiting the parties and their attorneys from speaking publicly about a pending case. But absent a gag order, and subject to some professional restraints concerning reasonableness, neither a prosecutor, the police, a defendant, or defense counsel are prohibited from speaking to the press.

Some states permit television cameras in courtrooms to provide real time and/or archived viewing of court proceedings, being careful not to let such activity interfere with the dignity of the proceedings. The federal **district courts** do not. All of the federal courts of appeals, with one exception, and the Supreme Court of the United States bar live video transmission or recording of their proceedings, although a transcript is subsequently available. The one exception is the US Court of Appeals for the Ninth Circuit (which includes California and several other western states), which live streams and video archives its proceedings.

In federal courts (state laws vary), **victims** have limited rights granted by the F. R. Crim. P. and statutes. Under Rule 60, victims have a right to reasonable notice of a public proceeding involving the crime. The **Crime Victims' Rights Act**, 18 U.S.C. § 3771(a)(4), grants crime victims the right "to be reasonably heard at sentencing" and the right to "full and timely restitution." In some circumstances, victims may attend and be heard at proceedings regarding release of the defendant, pleas, or sentencing. But otherwise, they have no formal status in a criminal proceeding, do not participate in a trial as a party, and cannot veto a plea agreement or sentence. A victim may often be a witness at trial against the defendant, but the decision whether to ask a victim to testify is made exclusively by the prosecutor, and the victim is subject to the same rules as any other witness, including cross-examination by the defendant's attorney. In many states, evidentiary rules applicable to sex offenses may limit cross-examination of a victim, often to exclude evidence of the victim's sexual history. If a victim seeks compensation from a defendant, he proceeds through a civil proceeding that is entirely separate from the criminal trial; a criminal jury does not award damages to a victim. Guilty plea agreements sometimes include a provision obligating a defendant to provide victim compensation.

14 SENTENCING

If a defendant is found guilty at trial or pleads guilty, the court will set a date for sentencing—in the federal system usually a month or two after the verdict or plea. As a technical matter, no **judgment** of conviction has been entered until a sentence is imposed.

Traditionally, sentencing has been considered a matter allocated principally to the discretion of the judge. Under a regime known as **indeterminate sentencing**, the judge could impose any sentence from zero to the maximum set by the legislature for the crime, without any meaningful appellate review. This led to a perceived problem of disparate sentencing, under which different judges might give wildly different sentences for comparable cases, a problem exacerbated by the absence of any need for a judge to explain or justify the sentence, and the absence of appellate review. In the 1980s, the federal Congress and a number of states introduced measures designed to structure sentencing to make the process more coherent and diminish—or at least channel—the discretion left to trial judges. As a result, sentencing now reflects inputs from a number of different sources, which in the federal system may include

- trial judges, who are still the primary decision makers on individual sentences;
- legislators, who have limited the discretion of judges by adopting **guidelines** for the imposition of sentences, and **mandatory minimum sentences** that may apply in certain circumstances;
- prosecutors, whose position on sentencing has always been an input, but who now may have greater impact on sentencing through their

enhanced role under sentencing guidelines and regarding mandatory minimums, especially through **negotiated outcomes;**

- juries, who under relatively recent jurisprudence are involved in a very limited, but nonetheless important, set of circumstances;
- victims, who under some circumstances have a limited right to be heard on sentencing; and
- appellate judges, who now engage in a limited but nonetheless significant review of sentences.

A. THE TRADITIONAL APPROACH AND THE ROLE OF TRIAL JUDGES

Prior to the 1980s, trial judges had near-total discretion to impose any sentence they wished between zero and the statutory maximum. Even under new regimes designed to curb judicial discretion, sentencing judges remain responsible for managing the sentencing process, and are crucial decision makers in sentencing.

Sentencing judges approach each defendant as an individual: they attempt to understand the specific criminal conduct involved, as well as the defendant's broader life circumstances, and then attempt to determine a sentence that responds to that particular case. It may be said that they evaluate "culpability" (the degree of the convicted defendant's personal responsibility) as well as "harm" (the damage to society). To do so, a federal judge relies significantly on a **presentence investigation report** (PSI) prepared by the office of the **US Probation and Pretrial Services System** (which functions within the US court system) in that district. The PSI will include the fruits of the pretrial services officer's interview with the defendant and any inquiry made into the defendant's background, including prior criminal history. The PSI is submitted to both the prosecutor and the defendant's attorney for review (either of whom may contest any perceived inaccuracy in it at or prior to the sentencing), and the pretrial service officer may meet confidentially with the judge to discuss the report. Most importantly, in federal cases the PSI will provide the officer's calculation under the **Federal Sentencing Guidelines** discussed later. If the ultimate sentence includes or consists of supervised **probation**, the Probation and Pretrial Services office will supervise it.

The imposition of the sentence by the judge takes place in public court. The judge will ask both the prosecutor and the defense attorney if they have any comments on the PSI or on the sentence generally. If the sentence is the result of a negotiated guilty plea, the parties may have few or no comments to add to the plea agreement. But in many circumstances, the prosecutor and the defendant may disagree about the appropriate calculation under the applicable guidelines, and discussion on that subject may be extended. In unusual circumstances, a judge may conclude that he cannot appropriately make the determinations or classifications required by the guidelines without further information, and on infrequent occasions the judge may conduct a hearing on such issues. Before the judge imposes the sentence, he will ask the defendant if he wishes to be heard, and most defendants briefly address the court, often in order to express contrition. The judge will generally ask the defendant to stand when the sentence is pronounced. After imposition of the sentence, the judge will inform the defendant of his right to appeal, and the sentence will be recorded in a formal **judgment**.

If the defendant is already in custody at the time of sentence and is sentenced to a term that he has not already served (it is not uncommon, particularly in some state courts, to impose a sentence of **time served**, which will result in the defendant's immediate release), he is likely to remain in custody, now serving the sentence that has been imposed. If the defendant has remained at liberty prior to sentence, the prosecutor may ask that a defendant sentenced to a prison term begin serving it immediately. The judge must then determine whether to allow the defendant to remain at liberty for a brief period to organize his affairs before surrendering, or alternatively to remain free pending an appeal. The judge's decision on this issue will be guided by the length of the prison term, the seriousness of the offense, the possibility of flight, and the apparent strength of likely issues on appeal. A denial of release pending appeal may be immediately appealed to the court of appeals.

B. LEGISLATIVE "REFORM" OF SENTENCING

Concerned with disparate sentencing, and at a time when a "war on crime" was politically sensitive, Congress adopted the **Sentencing Reform Act of 1984**, which is applicable to federal criminal cases. This legislation, and similar efforts in many states, have had a profound—and controversial—impact on sentencing procedures and outcomes. Their principal innovations were to establish the **Federal Sentencing Guidelines** to channel or limit judges' discretion in virtually all cases, and to impose mandatory minimum sentences for certain categories of cases.

The core concept of the federal Sentencing Reform Act was relatively straightforward, at least in theory. The Act first established a Sentencing Commission that was tasked with reviewing data relating to the sentences imposed under a variety of crimes and in different circumstances, and to propose an analytical matrix—the Federal Sentencing Guidelines—to apply to each case going forward. The Guidelines require the judge in each case (with the help of the Probation and Pretrial Services office) to engage in a calculation based on a number of factors. These factors begin with the categorization of the criminal law of which the defendant has been convicted by its relative severity, and then include a number of factors specific to each case. This will include the severity of the crime, often as determined by specific metrics (the amounts, as well as the kind, of drugs in a narcotics case; the amount of money involved in a fraud or other business case), as well as specific facts relating to the defendant, including his background, the degree to which he has expressed contrition or remorse, and other factors. Recidivism is a major factor. From this calculation emerges a "target" range of sentences. As originally envisioned, once this range was established, judges retained the discretion to impose any sentence within it, and any sentence within this range could not be appealed. If a judge found that in any individual case a so-called "departure" above or below the range was appropriate, he could impose such a sentence—but only upon stating the reasons for the departure, a decision that could be reviewed on appeal. (A prosecutor could appeal a "downward departure," and the defendant could appeal an "upward departure.") The legality of the Guidelines has been challenged in court on a number of bases, and in 2005, the Supreme Court decided in *United States v. Booker*, 543 U.S. 220 (2005) that the

Guidelines could not be considered mandatory on either trial or appellate judges. As a result, the Guidelines are used by trial judges as the principal framework under which they determine sentences, but they are free to depart from them. And on appeal, under *Booker*, the appellate court can review any sentence for its "reasonableness," and invalidate a sentence if it finds that the sentence was "unreasonable" under all the circumstances.

The overall practical effect of the Sentencing Guidelines has almost certainly been to increase the length of sentences generally, which appears in a number of statistics compiled from court records, as well as in the number of people incarcerated in federal (and many state) prisons, which has skyrocketed since the Federal Sentencing Guidelines (or their state analogues) were adopted. (The level of such incarceration, both as an absolute number and as a relative proportion of the population in many countries, is set forth in Figures 2 and 3 in Chapter 1.)

Of similar significance is the widespread adoption of **mandatory minimum sentencing**, pursuant to which legislators direct that under specified circumstances—such as the severity of the crime, whether or not the defendant was guilty of prior infractions, and other inputs—the sentencing judge lacks discretion to impose a sentence lower than a stated mandatory minimum. Some of these mandatory minimums are in fact quite high and can amount to twenty years or even higher imprisonment. They apply most frequently, but not entirely, in the area of narcotics. The role of mandatory minimum sentences in plea negotiations was discussed in Chapter 11.C, and their baleful effect on the administration of justice will be mentioned again in the Conclusion, Chapter 19.

In addition to determining the appropriate sentence on each **count**, judges may have discretion to provide that sentences on more than one count be **concurrent** or **consecutive** with each other, which in the latter instance may easily result in the imposition of a sentence exceeding the maximum for any one count.

C. THE ROLE OF PROSECUTORS

Even during the era of **indeterminate sentencing**, prosecutors had a significant role in sentencing. As set forth in Chapter 11.A, during

guilty plea negotiations prosecutors can negotiate the position they will take at sentencing, and under Rule 11(c)(1)(C) of the Federal Rules of Criminal Procedure can even agree on a specific sentence, although that sentence requires approval by the judge (absent which the plea may be withdrawn). Absent an agreement, the prosecutor can be heard at sentence to advocate for a high (or possibly a low) sentence, although absent agreement a prosecutor can also take no position on sentencing at all. The arrival of the Federal Sentencing Guidelines (and state analogues) and of mandatory minimums, however, has given prosecutors significantly greater impact on sentencing, which has fundamentally changed the dynamics of criminal justice.

As noted, the Sentencing Guidelines were originally conceived as mandatory, and even after *Booker* remain the fundamental basis for the calculation of sentences; as further noted, under many circumstances they will lead to the imposition of long sentences. But the Guidelines also give prosecutors the means to radically change the sentencing analysis applicable to a particular defendant who **cooperates** with the prosecutor, usually by providing evidence against others. If a prosecutor, in her sole discretion, determines that a defendant has provided "substantial assistance" to the prosecutor, she can file a motion pursuant to Section 5K1.1 of the Federal Sentencing Guidelines (known as a **5 K motion**) prior to sentencing, stating that the defendant has cooperated. The filing of such a motion allows the court to impose whatever sentence it deems appropriate, even if it is below the "range" determined by the Guidelines. (Even after the imposition of sentence, Rule 35 of the F. R. Crim. P. provides that the prosecutor may retroactively seek to reduce a sentence based upon receipt of "substantial assistance" from a convicted defendant.) The "5 K" provision in the Sentencing Guidelines is an extremely important part of a federal prosecutor's arsenal, and is the bedrock of an investigative approach, common in the United States, to prosecute lesser figures and use the sentencing provisions as pressure to obtain their cooperation in providing information and, if necessary, testimony against others.

The phenomenon of **mandatory minimum sentencing** has had the (probably unintended) consequence of giving prosecutors even greater powers over sentencing. This is because of the essentially unreviewable discretion that prosecutors have over the **charging deci-sion**, as set forth in Chapter 6.A. In a given case, a prosecutor may decide—and can negotiate with the defendant over—not only whether or not to include the highest possible charge against a defendant, but also whether to include all of the available *facts* in a charge. For exam-ple, a defendant from whom a large quantity of narcotics has been seized may face the risk of a very high mandatory minimum if charged with trafficking in the total amount seized. But the prosecutor has full authority to elect to charge the defendant with trafficking in some, but not all, of the narcotics actually seized, which may lower or even eliminate the mandatory minimum. The prosecutor may elect to do so for benign policy reasons: in an effort to address a level of incarcera-tion that was widely viewed as excessive, during the administration of President Obama, former Attorney General Eric Holder directed pro-secutors not to automatically charge defendants with narcotics offenses based on the real amounts involved if charging a lower amount would result in a more reasonable sentence in light of the criminal history of the defendant and other factors. While this goal was laudable (and fairly effective), the ability to negotiate over the factual parameters of a crime frees prosecutors to use their charging decisions to put con-siderable—perhaps even intolerable—pressure on defendants to plead guilty. For example, a prosecutor may offer to charge a lesser amount of narcotics that, upon conviction, would lead to a low or even no mandatory minimum—but only if the defendant foregoes trial and pleads guilty, absent which the defendant may face charges based on the full amount of narcotics seized, which would result in a high man-datory minimum if the defendant is convicted. In either case, the prosecutor would need to prove the offense charged in order to obtain a conviction, and, in most cases, the sentencing judge would have the discretion to impose a high sentence in any event. But the ability to negotiate over whether a defendant is even charged with a crime that, if proven, leads to a high mandatory sentence creates a huge disparity in bargaining power. The implications of this practice are troubling, for reasons summarized in the Conclusion in Chapter 19.

Because these provisions can be both automatic and rigid, the drafters included some elements of flexibility in the form of so-called **safety valves**, which are provisions that in very limited circumstances a judge may make findings that a specific defendant's situation should not be subject to mandatory minimum sentences. Those provisions, however, have been very limited indeed and are themselves inflexible; relatively few defendants meet their prerequisites. In December 2018, Congress adopted and the president signed some reform in this area, included in a criminal justice reform package known informally as the **First Step Act**. The Act reflects some incipient bipartisan unease about the size of US prison populations, often caused by concern about their costs. Among its features is some modest increase in the applicability of safety valves. Since the legislation will take effect only prospectively, it may take a few years to determine its impact on sentencing.

D. THE ROLE OF JURIES IN SENTENCING

Jurors do not decide sentences, and when they deliberate to determine the guilt or nonguilt of the defendant as set forth in Chapter 13.F, they must not speculate on what sentence, if any, may be imposed (and the possible range of sentences, or even the existence of a mandatory minimum, will not have been communicated to jurors). Some relatively recent decisions, however, require jury input in sentencing under certain limited circumstances.

Some statutory regimes set a maximum sentence, but provide that the maximum is raised if certain facts—such as a prior conviction, or particularly egregious circumstances such as violence—are present. And as noted, under certain circumstances, a mandatory minimum may be applicable. Under a series of decisions leading to *United States v. Booker*, 543 U.S. 220 (2005), the Supreme Court has held that other than with respect to a prior conviction (which can be irrefutably established by a copy of its formal judgment), any factual determination that may result in a mandatory minimum or in an increased maximum must be made by a jury.

Separately, in those states and in federal cases where the **death penalty** is sought, after conviction a jury must be asked to determine the appropriateness of a death sentence based on their evaluation of factors, known as "aggravators" and "mitigators," specific to the defendant. The procedures for such jury consultation (including whether the jury verdict on the sentence must be **unanimous** or not) varies considerably from jurisdiction to jurisdiction.

E. VICTIMS

Unlike in some European and other regimes, victims do not have a formal role in a criminal prosecution (see Chapter 13.J). A criminal conviction will not include a judgment in favor of a victim, who must pursue compensation in a separate, civil proceeding, although at the discretion of a prosecutor and with the approval of a judge, a negotiated outcome such as a guilty plea may include restitution or reimbursement to a victim (see Chapter 11.C). As a result, at sentencing a victim generally at most has a right to submit to the judge his views on the appropriate sentence, and even in the absence of a statutory provision to this effect, most judges will allow victims to be heard.

F. THE ROLE OF APPELLATE JUDGES

As noted previously, during the era of indeterminate sentencing, appellate courts had virtually no role in sentencing because sentences were considered to be solely within the discretion of the sentencing judge. The move to bring greater consistency to sentences has changed the role of appellate judges to some degree. The original concept of the Federal Sentencing Guidelines was that appellate judges would review any "upward" or "downward departures" from the then-mandatory guidelines. Since the *Booker* decision noted previously, appellate courts only review sentences for "reasonableness" (see Chapter 15.E).

Appellate courts, like sentencing judges at trial, are bound by statutory **mandatory minimum** provisions. In very exceptional cases, an appellate court occasionally finds that a mandatory minimum was so grossly disproportionate to the specific facts of the case as to be unconstitutional under the prohibition in the **Eighth Amendment** banning "cruel and unusual punishment."

15 APPEALS

Appellate courts play a major role in the administration of criminal justice in two ways: a person convicted of a crime can have his conviction reviewed for legal error by an appellate court to ensure that appropriate procedures were followed in his individual case, and appellate court decisions in criminal cases are **precedent** that contribute to the evolution and development of the **common law** of criminal procedures. This second point merits emphasis, because many very important aspects of criminal procedure can only be understood by being familiar with the recent decisions—and thus the common law—applicable to them. While US criminal procedures in general share many important characteristics, which this book attempts to summarize, they may vary among the various states, and even in the federal system the decisions in the various federal **courts of appeals** sometimes differ.

A. THE STRUCTURE OF APPELLATE REVIEW

In the federal system, appeals from one of the ninety-four **district courts** (where criminal trials are held) lie with the regional **court of appeals** for the circuit in which the district court is found (see Chapter 2.A). A decision from a federal court of appeals may be reviewed by the **Supreme Court**, but as noted, the Supreme Court controls its own caseload and generally decides only a handful of criminal procedure questions each year, generally when two or more of the courts of appeals disagree on a legal point of significance. The Supreme Court of the United States can also review a final decision from a state supreme court but only to determine if the state court judgment conforms with the US Constitution (See Chapter 2.A.).

The states vary in how they structure criminal appellate review. Each state has a "supreme court," although the highest court in the state is not always known by that name, and a state may establish an intermediary appellate court between the trial court and its supreme court. In New York, for example, appeals in criminal matters lie with the Appellate Division, of which there are four separate divisions; and some decisions from an Appellate Division may be heard by the state's highest court, which is called the New York Court of Appeals. See Chapter 2.A.

B. APPEALS PRIOR TO TRIAL

By far the most appeals in criminal matters are requests to review a conviction at the request of the convicted defendant, which are discussed in the next section. Sometimes, however, either the prosecution or the defendant may seek appellate review before a trial or even if no trial will take place. Such **interlocutory appeals** are strictly limited, especially in the federal courts; parties to a criminal proceeding in a trial court cannot normally ask an appellate court to intercede in a case prior to trial but can do so only if the trial court has made a decision that effectively ends or at least eviscerates a trial.

In relatively infrequent instances, a trial court may **dismiss** an indictment prior to trial, generally based on finding a legal bar such as an expired statute of limitations, a finding that the court is not competent to hear the matter, or ruling that the facts alleged in the indictment do not state a crime; such a dismissal, once final and conclusive in the trial court, can generally be appealed by the prosecutor. In other circumstances, a trial court may order the exclusion of significant evidence that the prosecutor intends to introduce at trial—often on the basis of an **exclusionary rule**, as set forth in Chapter 10.C. If the prosecutor deems that she cannot effectively proceed to trial without the suppressed evidence, she may ask the trial court to stay the trial proceedings so that she can pursue an **interlocutory appeal** to ask an appellate court to review the legal issue that led to the exclusion of evidence, sometimes on the implicit commitment that if the prosecutor does not prevail on the appeal, she will abandon the prosecution.

A defendant has virtually no avenues to appeal adverse decisions prior to—or during—a trial; rather, any claims of legal error must be **preserved** by making an appropriate objection so that in the event of a conviction, the appellate court can review the issue in the context of reviewing the conviction itself (see Chapter 15.D).

In federal courts, and some state courts, a defendant who has made an application to exclude crucial evidence or a legal argument directed to the prosecution as a whole but has failed to persuade the trial court to do so, may, with the agreement of the prosecutor, enter a **conditional plea** of guilty. F. R. Crim. P. 11(a)(2), for example, permits a guilty plea reserving the right to seek appellate review of the contested issue, where "[a] defendant who prevails on appeal may then withdraw the plea" (see Chapter 11.C).

Under very unusual circumstances, a party—either the prosecutor or a defendant—who claims that a trial judge simply lacked the power to act may seek a so-called **writ of mandamus** from an appellate court, seeking emergency review of a trial court decision. Recourse to this writ is strongly discouraged by the courts, especially in the federal system; they are very rarely issued, and the courts vigilantly restrict their use of the writ. The very few instances in which a mandamus writ has been successfully invoked generally involve situations where a trial judge entered an order that he lacked power to issue at all (as opposed to doing so on an erroneous basis, which would normally be reviewable after conviction) *and* where it is clear that an appeal after conviction would not effectively address the problem. As a recent example, one of the federal courts of appeals reviewed the refusal of a district court judge to accept an outcome negotiated by the parties; such a decision is not normally appealable and could not ultimately be raised in a post-trial appeal, but raised an important legal issue that the appellate court wished to reach

C. APPEALS AFTER CONVICTION—PROCEDURES

If a trial ends in a complete **acquittal**, the case is effectively over. A prosecutor may not appeal or seek other review of an acquittal, nor may she inquire of the jury about the reasons underlying a decision to acquit in an effort to change the verdict. As noted in Chapter 12, an acquitted defendant is protected against reprosecution by the principle of **double jeopardy**, at least for now limited by the "single sovereign" rule.

If a defendant is convicted, even on a single **count**, he has a right to seek review of that conviction from an appellate court (and perhaps two hierarchical courts, depending on the structure of a state's court system). An appeal is commenced by filing a notice of appeal with the trial court, which then transfers the formal **record**—which includes all papers filed in the trial court, together with the verbatim **transcript** of proceedings—to the appropriate appellate court. The filing of a notice of appeal does not automatically suspend the immediate obligation of a defendant to serve a sentence. A convicted defendant sentenced to a term of imprisonment may ask the trial court, in the first instance, to stay the immediate exercise of sentence until the appellate court has ruled (and may immediately ask an appellate court to do so if an application for a stay is denied); the trial court may well stay the exercise of the sentence if the defendant can articulate a plausible ground for appellate review and can demonstrate no risk of flight or danger to the community (see Chapter 13.F).

The general practice for an appeal in the federal and most state systems is that the appellant files a written memorandum (or "brief"), the appellee (that is, the prosecutor in those instances where a convicted defendant is appealing) files a responsive brief, and the appellant generally is permitted a short written reply. In most but not all instances, the court will schedule oral argument where counsel for the parties present their points and respond to questions from the court. Such arguments are often limited to fifteen or twenty minutes per side, although they may be longer in complex cases or where there are multiple parties. The judges will have read the briefs, and counsel are not expected to repeat what is already expressed in them; oral arguments often serve as an opportunity for the judges to ask questions. In the federal system, appeals are heard by a panel of three judges chosen at random from the judges of the federal **court of appeals** for that circuit (although occasionally federal judges from another court are invited to sit as a "visiting judge"), who will generally sit together for several days or a week and hear arguments on all appeals (civil and administrative, as well as criminal) set for argument during that period. In some instances where the issues are simple and clear, the panel may "rule from the bench"—that is, announce their decision immediately after argument—which may or may not be followed by a written opinion. In most instances, however, the judges will indicate that they are "reserving decision," which will be announced in a written (and public) opinion. The length of time that judges spend deliberating and writing their opinions varies tremendously and may be as few as several days or may take several months or even a year or more. The date when a decision will issue is generally not made public in advance, so that the parties—and the public—only learn of it from the official announcement by the court on the day the decision is released.

Most appellate opinions are authored by a single judge whose name will appear as the author, although courts can also issue opinions written *per curiam* ("by the court") without attributing authorship to a specific judge. The judges who agree with the principal opinion may simply "join" it. On occasion, a judge may join the principal opinion, or at least agree with its result, but also file a "concurring opinion" that may add some additional reasoning but reaches the same result as the principal opinion. A judge may file a "dissenting" opinion if he would reach a result different from the one reached by the others, stating the grounds for his disagreement, in which case the principal opinion will be known as the "majority" opinion.

A party whose arguments have been rejected by a panel of judges on appeal may, in the federal system, file a "motion for rehearing," which asks that the same judges review their decision, generally on the ground that there is a key point that they had missed or misunderstood; and they may also file a "suggestion for rehearing *en banc*," which if granted will result in the issue being argued to a group including *all* of the active judges in the court. Rehearing and rehearing *en banc* are infrequent.

D. APPEALS AFTER CONVICTION—SCOPE OF REVIEW

It is essential to understand the scope of appellate review—that is, what the appellate courts do and do not decide. Most fundamentally, appellate courts do not revisit or remake the essential decision reached in the trial court—that is, to determine whether or not the defendant is guilty. Rather, their focus is on the fairness of the trial proceedings that led to a conviction. Appellate review is thus limited to legal issues and to decisions made by the trial judge that may have had an impact on the fairness of the trial. The governing principle is that the "finders of fact" (principally the jury but in some circumstances the trial judge) were the only ones able to make evaluations concerning the weight of the evidence and in particular the credibility of the witnesses. Appellate judges thus cannot substitute their views on factual issues for findings or determinations made by the trial judge or the jury if the procedures for doing so were fair and appropriate.

A convicted defendant who appeals on the ground that the evidence was insufficient to support a conviction thus has a steep burden. When asked to review factual sufficiency, the appellate judges will "view the evidence in the light most favorable to the government" by assuming that witnesses who had testified in support of conviction had been found credible, and that the jury had given the maximum weight to evidence—and drawn the maximum appropriate inference from circumstances—that they reasonably could. In those instances where a defendant either testified or called witnesses on his behalf but was nonetheless convicted, the appellate judges will assume that those witnesses were disbelieved or had no weight and cannot "balance" their testimony against testimony supporting prosecution. If the judges conclude that a rational jury "could have found" facts sufficient to support conviction, they cannot vacate the conviction for want of evidence, even if they believe that the jury was mistaken. It is thus possible for an appellate court to reverse a conviction on the grounds of insufficient evidence, but these instances are uncommon. The standard for appellate review of the sufficiency of the evidence is essentially the same as that applied by a trial judge faced with a **motion for a judgment of acquittal,** as discussed in Chapter 13.F.3.

Some states provide somewhat greater latitude to appellate judges in this respect. In New York, for example, appellate judges can—and occasionally but not frequently do—vacate a conviction "in the interest of justice" if they are convinced that a miscarriage of justice occurred, even without finding a specific legal error.

Appellate reviews thus tend to focus on legal issues, of which two predominate.

First, appellate courts are often asked to review decisions made by the trial court on the **admissibility** of evidence during trial, often decisions to admit evidence favorable to the prosecution, but sometimes decisions to exclude evidence offered by the defense. When asked to review an evidentiary decision, an appellate court must address three questions before reversing the conviction:

- Was the issue *preserved?* At trial, a defense counsel faced with an adverse ruling on an issue of evidentiary admissibility must be vigilant to state that he "objects" to the decision and state with some precision exactly what he is asking the court to do, such as to exclude the evidence entirely or issue a "limiting" instruction to the jury to cabin the use of the evidence. Absent such an objection, on appeal the appellate court may review an issue that "was not brought to the [trial] court's attention" only if it is "plain error," which is defined in Rule 52(b) of the Federal Rules of Criminal Procedure as an "error that affects substantial rights"—a difficult burden to satisfy. Appellate judges often refuse to review a trial court's ruling on evidence (and some other issues) on the ground that no (or an insufficient) objection to it was made.
- Was the trial court's decision *correct?* Many appellate decisions address in some detail the applicable **rules of evidence** (such as the **Federal Rules of Evidence** in federal courts), and their interpretation of evidentiary rules contributes to the important **common law** on this subject.
- Was the error (if any) *harmless?* F. R. Crim. P. Rule 52(a) provides that "[a]ny error, defect, irregularity or variance that does not affect substantial rights must be disregarded." In the area of evidentiary decisions, an appellate court may well find that a decision made by the trial court was technically wrong but because of its relative insignificance—particularly if the evidence of guilt is strong—may conclude that the error was harmless.

The second area where one sees significant discussion in criminal appellate decisions is the review of the **instructions to the jury**. Jurors

deliberate alone—without any judicial participation or supervision—
yet must scrupulously apply the law (see Chapter 13.F). Their understanding of the law that they are obligated to apply is based on the
formal instructions given to them by the judge, as noted previously,
after the end of the presentation of evidence and immediately before
they commence their secret deliberations. Particularly because no one
is permitted to inquire *how* the jurors actually reached their decision in
an effort to overturn their verdict, it follows that if the instructions were
materially incorrect, the conviction generally must be vacated and the
case sent back for a new trial since one cannot know if the jury
convicted on a legally permissible basis or not. To qualify as a basis
for reversal, an error in instructions must generally have been preserved
by an appropriate objection to the trial court, but courts are somewhat
less likely to invoke the notion of **harmless error** if there was any real
possibility that the jury may have been confused about the legal principles they were to apply.

In addition to these two grounds for review, an appellant's lawyer
may search the **record** and raise any issue where he can plausibly claim
that the procedures were erroneous, at least if he can surmount the
"preservation" and "harmless error" hurdles. Errors in the jury selection process, extreme conduct by a trial judge or a prosecutor, inappropriate curtailment of witness examination, selective or biased
prosecution, these and many other possible claims may be developed
by resourceful counsel reviewing a trial record. But compared with
appeals related to evidentiary issues and jury instructions, they are less
frequent. And in any event, a defendant in most instances would still
need to show that the error complained of was preserved and was not
harmless.

E. APPEALS AFTER CONVICTION—SENTENCING

Traditionally, the determination of sentence was considered to fall
within the discretion of the sentencing judge and could not be
appealed. In the federal system, the **Sentencing Reform Act of
1984** imposed a fundamentally new regime for the calculation of sentences where trial judges must apply carefully constructed **Federal**

Sentencing Guidelines, discussed in Chapter 14.B, that are designed to channel the exercise of their discretion and thereby achieve greater uniformity in sentences. As noted in Chapter 14.B, subsequent Supreme Court decisions ruled that the guidelines cannot be considered mandatory, but that courts must carefully consider them in determining the appropriate sentence. On appeal of a federal conviction, the appellate courts will also not view the guideline calculations as mandatory; they generally give deference to sentences that fall within them, although the ultimate test on appeal of a sentence is whether the sentence imposed was "reasonable" under all the circumstances. Appellate review of sentences in state courts varies widely.

F. APPEALS AFTER CONVICTION—THE DISPOSITION BY THE APPELLATE COURT

As noted, appellate judges do not substitute their view of the facts—or of the guilt of the defendant—for the findings made by the jury and/or the trial judge. As a result, an appellate court does not issue its own criminal judgment of either "guilty" or "not guilty" as is issued in a trial court. Rather, if the court concludes that no error undermined the legal viability of the judgment of conviction, that **judgment** is "affirmed" and the trial court's judgment of conviction remains in effect. If, however, the appellate court concludes that the conviction was affected by error, it will "reverse" the decision of the trial court and most often "vacate" the conviction, and then "remand" to the trial court to carry out the next steps made necessary by the appellate court's opinion. In many instances where the appellate court has found an error in the admissibility of evidence or in the instructions, for example, it will vacate the judgment of conviction and "remand for a new trial," which permits (but does not obligate) the prosecutor to seek a new trial. Under unusual circumstances, if the court concludes that the evidence at trial was insufficient to support a conviction under the exigent standard noted previously, it may "remand" with directions to **dismiss** the indictment, which will signify the **acquittal** of the defendant. If the appellate court finds error in the proceedings before the grand jury that were sufficiently important to invalidate the indictment issued by it, the court may order the dismissal of the indictment, in some instances leaving open the possibility that the matter will be presented to a new grand jury.

G. COLLATERAL REVIEW

In the vast majority of cases that lead to a conviction after trial, an affirmance by an appellate court will be the end of the matter. As noted in Chapter 2.A.2, Supreme Court review is very infrequent. Further, as also noted in Chapter 2.A, the federal courts do not systematically review decisions in state courts; thus a conviction affirmed by a state's highest court is very likely to be final and conclusive.

If a defendant finds new evidence that casts serious doubt on the justice of his conviction—or, more spectacularly, tends to prove that he is innocent—he may pursue avenues available in the court where he had been convicted to review the case. DNA techniques, for example, have in some instances permitted a convicted defendant to reopen his case, sometimes because the new evidence shows that someone other than the convicted defendant was in fact the perpetrator. The standards for such review are quite high, and judges strongly resist simply relitigating a trial; a convicted defendant must show that the proffered evidence is truly "new" and was not available during trial, and that it raises a real question about his guilt. Rule 33 of the Federal Rules of Criminal Procedure provides that a "court may vacate any judgment and grant a new trial if the interest of justice so requires," and specifies that if based upon the discovery of new evidence, such a motion must be made within three years of verdict. The rules on this subject, including time periods, vary tremendously among the various states.

In exceptional circumstances, a defendant can seek what is called **collateral review** of a state court judgment by means of a **writ of habeas corpus**. Each state may have its own procedures for such post-conviction, post-appeal review, which vary tremendously. The federal provisions for post-conviction review of state court convictions, found in 28 U.S.C. § 2254, provide that relief may be granted if a federal court concludes that the defendant "is in custody in violation of the Constitution or laws or treaties of the United States."

The historic basis for federal *habeas corpus* is the belief that any conviction obtained in violation of the federal **Constitution** should be capable of review by a federal court. This remedy has proved to be controversial for two principal reasons. The first is simply the notion of finality—that once a defendant has had a fair trial and an appeal, he should not be able to continue to litigate issues already decided. And the second is the issue of state sovereignty—a resistance of some states to have decisions of their courts reviewed by federal courts. As a result, resort to collateral review has been limited both by statute and by judicial interpretation so that it occurs only in limited circumstances. Review by *habeas corpus* is certainly not available as an additional appeal or type of review applicable in every case. Rather, it is designed to correct state court judgments that have clearly violated established federal constitutional principles, often where it appears that a state has systematically been ignoring **precedent** established by the Supreme Court. The federal statute governing this remedy provides that it is available only after the applicant has "exhausted the remedies in the courts of the State" where he is held—including any remedy for collateral, postconviction review—or can demonstrate that such recourse would be fruitless. Therefore, a convicted defendant seeking a federal review of the conviction pursuant to this remedy must first raise all issues in the courts of the state where he was convicted. This requirement, in essence, allows the state courts to manage the record that could ultimately be provided to a federal court. For example, a state court hearing a claim for postconviction relief may hold a hearing and find that the proof upon which it is based is unreliable, or that the witnesses supporting it were incredible, which will create a difficult barrier for federal relief. Indeed, a strong presumption of regularity applies to the state court proceedings, and factual findings made there cannot easily be reviewed in federal court pursuant to this writ. ("[A] determination of a factual issue made by a State court shall be presumed to be correct. The applicant shall have the burden of rebutting the presumption of correctness by clear and convincing evidence . . . .")

One area where collateral review is often sought is in the imposition of the **death penalty,** which is now enforced in only a relatively small number of states (and occasionally, though very infrequently, in federal cases). Because of the regularity of death-row inmates' recourse to federal courts to review state court convictions, Congress in 1996 adopted the **Antiterrorism and Effective Death Penalty Act,** which purports to "streamline" federal collateral review in this area but in reality makes them more difficult by imposing time limits and essentially limiting each convicted defendant to a single attempt to obtain review, along with other procedural restrictions. As a result, collateral review of death penalties is a highly specialized and challenging area of advocacy. Notwithstanding these challenges, opponents of the death penalty do use the remedy to chip away at death penalty convictions where a federal court finds the procedures adopted in state court to be constitutionally wanting. For example, federal courts have in some instances found that state courts had not appropriately respected the *Brady* and *Giglio* rules—as noted in Chapter 10.B.3, the Constitution requires prosecutors to share with the defense material that might be exculpatory or would tend to undermine the prosecution's proof—and have occasionally vacated convictions on that basis. A vacation of a conviction on such a basis generally leaves the state free to prosecute the defendant again, since the collateral review does not normally lead to a judgment that the defendant is "not guilty," but only that he had been unfairly convicted.

Separate from the judicial system as such is the power to issue a **pardon,** which eradicates a conviction, and **commutation,** which relieves a convicted defendant from serving all or part of a sentence. Both are a form of **clemency** exercised by the executive branch. The President of the United States is empowered by the Constitution to pardon or commute federal (but not state) crimes. The various states have different procedures; in most, the governor has a form of pardon or commutation power, although in some states the power is allocated to an agency or board.

16 CORPORATE CRIMINAL RESPONSIBILITY

Corporate criminal responsibility refers to the legal principles that determine whether a corporation (or other nonpersonal entity) can be convicted of a crime. While those principles may not strictly be considered a question of "procedure," they have a very strong impact on criminal investigations in the United States. The principles applied in federal courts in the United States differ from those in many other countries—and, in fact, from principles applied in several of the states.

No federal statute defines or sets generally applicable standards for corporate criminal responsibility; rather, the law applicable to this issue is mostly a development of the **common law**. The federal approach is based on the notion of *respondeat superior*, which is a principle found in the law of torts rather than criminal law. The adoption of the *respondeat superior* principle to criminal proceedings derives from a 1909 decision of the Supreme Court which held that under a specific statute so providing, a corporation could be convicted of a crime. This holding has subsequently been applied, with little analysis, to federal criminal statutes generally, even if the statute is entirely silent on whether it was intended to apply to corporations. The principle is very broadly applied in criminal cases. A classic statement of the principle is that a corporation "may be held criminally liable for the acts of any of its agents [who] (1) commit a crime (2) within the scope of employment (3) with the intent to benefit the corporation." All three parts of this formulation have been expansively interpreted. Particularly important is the interpretation that "scope of employment" means "apparent authority" rather than "actual authority." An employee acting outside of the sphere of his formal authority may nonetheless "bind" the corporation if his motive included an interest to benefit it. As a result, unlike in some other countries, there is no "**compliance** defense" that would allow a company to defend itself by showing that the employee or agent in question acted without formal authority and in violation of explicit company policy or rules.

In 1962, an influential (but unofficial) think tank, the American Law Institute, promulgated a **Model Penal Code** (MPC) to provide guidance to legislators on criminal law principles. In Section 2.01, the MPC provides that a corporation is responsible only for acts "authorized, requested, commanded, performed or recklessly tolerated by the board of directors or by a high managerial agent acting in behalf of the corporation." This formulation—which is closer to the principles adopted by several countries in Europe—has never been adopted by the federal courts, and has been followed by legislatures or courts in only a minority of the states.

The protection against **self-incrimination** available to individuals under the **Fifth Amendment** does not apply to corporations, and thus corporations can be forced—often by **subpoena**—to produce documents and other information that incriminate not only the corporation itself but also its officers and employees. In fact, in many regulated industries, a company may have formal public disclosure obligations that make it particularly hard to keep knowledge of wrongdoing secret. A corporation can invoke the **attorney/client privilege** (see Chapter 18.B), so that its officers can consult with an attorney, knowing that no prosecutor or other third party can obtain access to those communications without consent. As noted in Chapter 17.A, in the United States in-house counsel employed as employees of a corporation are considered "lawyers" and as members of the legal profession, and communications between an in-house counsel and other officers or employees of a corporation may be protected by the attorney/client privilege. As emphasized in Chapter 17.B, invocation and protection of this privilege during an **internal investigation** can be tricky, especially in multinational contexts where the laws of more than one country may apply.

Implicitly recognizing that the threshold of conduct sufficient to subject a corporation to the risk of criminal conviction is quite low, and that the impact of a conviction may be felt by employees of a company who had nothing to do with an infraction, the **Department of Justice** has emphasized that it will not automatically prosecute all corporations suspected of having committed criminal acts, but rather has published guidelines—formally called the **Principles of Federal Prosecution Of Business Organizations**—which, while not binding, provide useful guidance to corporations and are designed to help them develop appropriate compliance programs and respond to the risk of criminal prosecution when one is discovered. Recent evolutions of these guidelines emphasize the DOJ's focus on prosecuting individuals responsible for corporate behavior rather than corporations themselves, at least in situations where the corporation cooperates with the prosecutor. In essence, the prosecutors use the powerful threat of corporate criminal responsibility as leverage to induce **cooperation** against individual officers and employees.

Largely because of these principles, and perhaps because juries might not be terribly sympathetic to them, few corporations go to trial when faced with a criminal investigation; as a practical matter, they are likely to do so only if they can show that no prosecutable crime occurred at all. In many instances, the corporation will at least explore a strategy of immediately learning as much as possible about the facts (often through an **internal investigation** as set forth in Chapter 17); evaluate the likely outcomes; explore the possibility of a **dismissal** or a **declination**; and if necessary consider taking advantage of the sentencing benefits of **self-reporting** and **cooperation**, or **negotiate** an outcome that avoids a trial, including a **deferred prosecution agreement**, as discussed in Chapter 11.D. Because it is much easier to prosecute companies (and harder to defend them) in the United States than in other countries, the Department of Justice has in some instances been notably aggressive—and often successful—in prosecuting non-American companies for violation of US laws, often taking advantage of expansive American principles of **territoriality**, as discussed in Chapter 2.A.1.

17 INTERNAL CORPORATE INVESTIGATIONS

In recent years, a virtual cottage industry has developed for law firms and other professionals to conduct **internal investigations** of corporations. Their conduct and use are now core elements of the criminal justice landscape for corporate (or "white collar") crime.

Such investigations vary in size and complexity, and often require detailed logistics. The basic goal is straightforward: to inquire into factual circumstances that may pose a risk of a criminal investigation or prosecution, and to report and (usually) analyze the legal risks. Such investigations generally consist of a systematic review of available documents, emails, and other evidence, and interviews with participants, among other sources of information. There are, however, several quite different contexts in which an internal investigation may be conducted; because these differences may bear on important legal principles, it is important to be clear exactly what kind of investigation is being considered before embarking on one in order to adopt an appropriate strategy and avoid the problems addressed in section B.

A. SOME DIFFERENT BASES FOR AN INTERNAL INVESTIGATION

At its simplest, an investigation may simply be part of the defense function. If a person (including a corporation) turns to a lawyer in order to obtain advice when faced with the possibility of a criminal investigation, the obligation of a lawyer to defend her client includes the professional duty to learn the facts, since without knowing the facts it is impossible to provide useful legal advice. In complex cases, conducting such an investigation calls for specialized skills, and often may include the retention of forensic, accounting, and other experts. When a factual investigation is conducted by or under the supervision of an attorney retained to advise or defend, in the United States such an inquest is carried out under the protection of professional privileges, including the **attorney/client privilege** and often the **work product privilege** (see Chapter 18.B). The inquiry is thus generally undertaken with the unambiguous understanding and commitment (and the professional obligation) that its contents and fruits will be kept strictly confidential to the client and not shared (at least without the client's express consent, as noted later) with any third party. This should be made unmistakably clear at the time of the attorney or law firm's retention.

Sometimes, however, corporations may ask attorneys and other professionals to conduct a factual inquiry that responds to two needs or concerns that are somewhat different from the request for legal advice and defense. First, the officers of a corporation owe a duty of care to the corporation and its shareholders, which includes a duty to be responsible for (and to minimize the impact of) any apparent wrongdoing within the company and often includes a duty to disclose to shareholders any material risks to the corporation's financial well-being. The company's auditors may be under professional restraints not to certify company records, or even under certain circumstances to insist on public disclosure, if they come across indications of wrongdoing. And sometimes highly publicized events may cause a corporation to make a public promise to conduct an investigation to be shared with the public. In such circumstances, the company may create an **independent investigation**—that is, an investigation not formally linked to the defense of the corporation as such, but rather conducted to establish a neutral presentation of the facts for one purpose or another. Independence (and the appearance of independence) may be sought, for example, when a law firm or other professional is formally retained not by the corporation itself but by its audit committee or a special board committee established for the purpose of investigating suspected or alleged wrongdoing. In this circumstance, the corporation may commit to make public the fruits of the investigation.

Second, and very differently, the corporation may arrive at a strategy that includes sharing the fruits of a factual investigation with a prosecutor or regulatory agency in the context of **negotiating** a favorable outcome. As set forth in Chapter 18.B, for example, corporations sometimes negotiate **deferred prosecution agreements ("DPAs") or non-prosecution agreements("NPAs")** with federal prosecutors (and, occasionally, with regulators) that may include an agreed-upon "statement of facts" to which the parties agree. Such a factual recitation is often based in significant part on an internal investigation conducted by the company, generally by attorneys retained to do so. Depending on the scope and timing of the negotiations, the prosecutor/regulator may be presented with a "report" compiled by attorneys upon its completion (and only after the client has agreed to the strategy of sharing this report for the purposes of negotiation, prior to which the report was still protected by the attorney/client privilege). Making such a decision to **waive** the protection of professional privileges is a consequential one, especially since such a waiver generally cannot be selective but will involve sharing all known and subsequently discovered information with a prosecutor, as set forth in Chapter 11.C.2 in the context of plea negotiations. In some instances, the company's attorneys may work out an agreement with prosecutors to do an internal investigation for the purpose of providing a basis for negotiation—that is, before a full investigation has even been completed. In such a case, a prosecutor may ask to review the plans for an investigation before its execution and offer comments designed to establish the conditions upon which it will find the investigation's ultimate report to be acceptable. In some circumstances a prosecutor may also insist on steps to avoid the internal investigation creating problems with her own investigation, such as requiring that certain witnesses not be interviewed until the prosecutor's investigators have had an opportunity to do so (a process known as **deconfliction**).

Confusion about the precise parameters and strategic goal of an investigation may lead to either or both of two problems. First, it is always crucial to understand and be vigilant about protecting the professional privileges that may apply to an inquiry, and to avoid their inadvertent waiver. An inquiry done for defense purposes should always be protected from compelled disclosure by the **attorney/client privilege** and probably by the **work product privilege** (see Chapter 18.B). At the other end of the spectrum, some forms of truly independent investigations may be designed from inception to result in a formal report that will be publicized or shared. (This may raise the question whether drafts or internal communications concerning the investigation are subject to compelled disclosure if demanded.) Sometimes, however, the distinction may not be so clear: an inquiry may begin as a defense function (and is thus covered by the attorney/client privilege) but shift its strategic basis if the client subsequently decides to negotiate with a prosecutor and directs its attorneys to share with a prosecutor the facts that they have learned during an inquiry. Conceptually, in the United States a client can formally **waive** its attorney/client privilege and thus authorize an attorney to share information that she otherwise would be professionally barred from sharing. A company (or person) generally cannot, however, make selective waiver; waving applicable professional privileges for selected pieces of information risks a claim that the privilege has been lost, and use of otherwise protected information for one purpose (such as in a civil litigation context) may undermine the right to rely on the privilege elsewhere.

Second, a lawyer must always be mindful of her credibility, especially when dealing with adversaries. If the lawyer is doing a true "independent" or public investigation, the parameters of her engagement may be to establish "what happened" rather than to develop the best defense for the client. A lawyer hired to advise and represent a client has a different obligation, which is to do her utmost to defend her client against possible charges; this never permits the attorney to share confidences or information obtained from the client without the client's express permission. As noted previously, a lawyer hired to defend a corporate client may be tasked by the client to explore a possible negotiated outcome and (following a decision made by the client to do so) to negotiate the best possible outcome among those that are available (see Chapter 11.C.2). Under US practice, a lawyer may be authorized by the client to share otherwise privileged information with a prosecutor or other adversary, and in some instances the information so shared may ultimately be part of a "statement of facts" for a negotiated disposition. In that circumstance, the lawyer risks being caught in a dilemma. The lawyer's professional obligation to the client is always to make "the best possible case" on the client's behalf, and certainly not to divulge facts that are hurtful to the client's case. But from a prosecutor's perspective, a negotiating dialogue with an attorney is only useful if the attorney is authorized to provide complete and accurate information, especially in response to questions; providing selective information (such as only facts that are helpful to the client) but refusing to provide more on request—or, worse, prevaricating—is inevitably counterproductive. There is only one way to avoid, or at least minimize, this difficult dilemma: the client should encourage and cooperate with its attorney to do a full and honest evaluation of the apparent risks of a situation under circumstances where that strategic process is clearly protected by the attorney/client and work-product privileges, and *then* make an informed decision about whether or not to enter into negotiations with a prosecutor or regulator on the basis of the facts, knowing that once such discussions begin it will be difficult or impossible to avoid complete disclosure. This is not simply a question of honesty and ethics, but also of sound strategy: prosecutors are not stupid, and an attempt to provide them with a factual recitation that is incorrect or incomplete will generally be discovered, almost inevitably leading to very negative consequences for the client.

B. SOME PITFALLS IN CONDUCTING AN INTERNAL INVESTIGATION

Corporate internal investigations of any sort may be logistically complex and require careful planning to avoid legal and strategic pitfalls. Several challenges arise frequently and should be evaluated and addressed in advance.

The Upjohn issue. Corporations can only act through their officers, employees, and other agents, and an attorney or other professional attempting to inquire into a corporation's conduct inevitably must interview the individuals who speak and act for it. In *Upjohn Co. v. United States*, 449 U.S. 383 (1981), the Supreme Court confirmed that the conduct of such interviews is covered by the **attorney/client privilege** protecting the corporation if the interview is part of a legal review by an attorney at the request of her client, the corporation. This principle applies not only to attorneys hired to conduct such an investigation, but also to **in-house counsel**, whose communications with corporate officers and employees are covered by the privilege. In many instances, such an investigation will also be covered by the **work product privilege**, discussed in Chapter 18.B. The *Upjohn* decision clearly emphasized, however, that the privilege in that situation "belongs" to the corporate client, not the person being interviewed, even if that person is an officer of the corporation and feels that the interview is confidential. From this, it follows that the corporation may later decide to waive its privilege and use the fruits of the interview in discussions with a prosecutor, leading to a **negotiated outcome** to its advantage—even if the person interviewed has not consented. The information the corporation so shares may even be turned over to a prosecutor and lead to prosecution of the employee. The *Upjohn* decision has led to two common practices, both salutary to preserving the privilege and avoiding potential conflicts. First, the attorney and her client should clearly designate who within the corporation is the lawyer's appropriate contact in discussions about the investigation and the defensive strategy in general, to ensure that all such communications remain clearly between the attorney and her "client," and thus protected by the attorney/client privilege. And second, it is considered appropriate practice to warn interviewees employed by the corporation—in what are popularly called "*Upjohn* warnings"—that the interviewing attorney is the attorney only for the corporation and not for the person being interviewed, and that the interview is *not* covered by a privilege upon which the interviewee can rely.

Ethical issues. By definition, a crime committed by a corporation necessarily involved individuals who acted for it, from which it follows that someone conducting an internal investigation may interview a person who is himself at risk of prosecution. Particularly since the fruits of that interview may be used by the corporation as it sees fit—including sharing it with a prosecutor in negotiating a consensual outcome, or even making the information public—the conduct of such an interview is fraught with ethical sensitivities for an attorney or other professional. It is imperative to advise a person at risk of self-incrimination to consult with his own attorney before participating in an interview. In such circumstances, individual interviewees often ask that the company pay for attorneys to advise them. The practices and local laws applicable to that question vary significantly; in some circumstances a company's by-laws may address the issue.

Cross-border investigations. The already complex matrix of principles applicable to internal investigations become more so when the investigation touches the laws and practices of more than one country, since professional and other rules applicable to the investigation may vary dramatically. An attorney conducting an investigation that concerns either a corporation or individual with non-US incorporation or citizenship, or involves documents or interviews located outside the United States, must be cognizant of possible risks posed by local laws and should consult with local counsel.

Among the variables are the following:

- *Whether the inquiry is protected by a professional privilege* and the procedures for preserving it. In the United States, virtually any genuine request to an attorney to obtain advice about an actual or potential risk of criminal prosecution is covered by at least the attorney/client privilege, and possibly the work product privilege as well. Further, an **in-house counsel** is considered a lawyer for this purpose, if she is performing law-related duties. Other countries are notably more restrictive about the circumstances under which a comparable privilege exists (see Chapter 18), and a communication considered "privileged" and thus protected against compelled production in the United States may lack such protection if non-US principles apply to the communication.
- *Local laws are different.* Recent decisions in the United Kingdom and Germany reflect principles quite different from those in the United States on whether an investigation conducted by and communications with an attorney relating to a corporate investigation are protected by a professional privilege. The Constitutional Court in Germany, for example, upheld the power of a local prosecutor to raid the local offices of an American law firm conducting an internal investigation in Germany and to seize the fruits of that investigation. The laws of all countries on these and similar issues may be nuanced and different; they are also subject to change and must be consulted frequently.
- *Whether and how material subject to a privilege can be used in adversarial negotiations.* It is commonplace in the United States that a client can waive the attorney/client privilege and authorize an attorney to share

privileged information with a third party, including an adversary in negotiations, but this is not uniformly the case elsewhere. In France, for example, it is clear since March 2016 (when the Paris Bar issued an opinion to this effect) that an *avocat* (French attorney) can conduct an internal investigation and that such an investigation is covered by the French near equivalent of the attorney/client privilege, but French professional rules normally do not allow an attorney to share such protected information with a third party, even with the client's consent or waiver. The Paris Bar has also issued specific guidelines on the conduct of investigative interviews in France.

- *Blocking statutes and other impediments to transfer.* A number of countries have laws that restrict transferring data or other information outside the country, at least unless the transfer is conducted pursuant to the terms of a formal cooperation mechanism such as a bilateral or multilateral treaty. These laws vary from country to country, but may restrict the ability of an attorney to conduct an investigation in one country where the goal is to present the information so obtained to an official in another country, particularly the United States. In addition, national and (especially in Europe) international standards of privacy and database management may restrict the transfer of data. Local workplace rules (including laws protecting employee rights) may also have an impact on an internal investigation.

18 PROFESSIONAL RESPONSIBILITY

During pretrial phases of a criminal matter, during trial, and on appeals, many of the principal participants—the prosecutors, defense counsel, and judges—all share a common profession: they are "lawyers" (or "attorneys," which is the same thing). The legal profession also includes **in-house counsel** for corporations if they are trained as lawyers and exercise legal functions within their corporate employers. Irrespective of their position or title, all such professionals must be licensed to practice law, and have a duty to act professionally and to respect certain ethical standards. Judges, prosecutors, and corporate counsel do not receive legal education or training that is different from those of other attorneys, and in fact lawyers shift from one role to another more frequently than is the case in many other countries.

As a practical matter, this means that during an adversarial criminal proceeding, the adversaries (prosecutors and defense counsel) and judges often may know each other, either from common education at the same or similar schools, or from acquaintanceship during the current or previous employment. For example, many (although far from all) defense counsel representing defendants were themselves at one point prosecutors. Most judges are required to have practiced in the legal profession (often as prosecutors or private counsel, occasionally as in-house counsel) for ten years prior to potential appointment (or, in those states where judges are elected, election) to the role of judge, and thereby will have made a number of professional relationships prior to becoming judges. All lawyers, regardless of their role, are encouraged to join in voluntary **bar associations**, as noted later, and are likely to develop professional relationships there as well. All of the positions relevant here, however, are "full-time" in the sense that absent highly unusual and rare exceptions, lawyers exercise one of the roles noted here at a time. In the federal system and in most states, working in a prosecutor's office, for example, is a full-time employment, and does not permit prosecutors to engage in other professional activities.

A. LICENSING REQUIREMENTS

Licensing of attorneys and supervision of the legal profession are left to the individual states, each of which may have different qualifications and procedures for obtaining a license to practice law. Generally, to obtain a license to practice law—often referred to as "becoming a member of the bar"—an individual must graduate from an accredited law school, pass a state "bar exam," and submit to a background check. In New York State, attorneys must complete fifty hours of pro bono legal services and undergo a review of their "character and fitness" to practice law, including scrutiny of prior disciplinary offenses and misconduct. Some states organize the licensing process through an "integrated bar," an association which all attorneys must join, whereas other states license attorneys through a state agency. In New York, attorneys are licensed through the court system, and "bar associations" are purely voluntary.

The individual federal courts have their own "bar," which an attorney must join in order to practice there, but these bars are maintained mostly for administrative purposes and are not really an additional or separate professional license. A federal **district court** bar is open to any attorney licensed to practice in that state; there are no additional licensing requirements to practice in federal courts. There is also no "federal bar" empowered to license attorneys; all attorneys must be licensed in a state, even if the attorney exclusively practices in federal court.

Separate from the licensing agency designated by each state, there are a number of **bar associations** that are voluntary and independent, and that lawyers may choose to join. These may be national (of which the largest and best known is the American Bar Association) or local (there are several such associations in New York, which are active at both the state and city level); every state and every large city will have at least one such voluntary association. Voluntary bar associations may also be specialized; for example, criminal defense practitioners may organize meetings and network through their own association. Unless the state has delegated specific authority to them, these associations engage in civil and educational activities, but do not have administrative responsibilities or authority over their members.

An attorney may be licensed by more than one state. Reciprocity rules vary, and an attorney licensed in one state may need to pass exams to practice in another state. An attorney who wishes to appear in a state where she is not admitted can ask to be admitted *pro hac vice*—that is, for a particular case, usually at the request and under the supervision of a locally admitted attorney. Rules that pertain to lawyers licensed in other countries also vary from state to state. In New York State, a lawyer admitted to practice law in another country can take the New York State bar exam (and thus become a New York lawyer upon successful completion of the exam and satisfaction of other requirements) if she either has a law degree from a "common law" country or, alternatively, a law degree from a non–common law country together with at least a one-year degree in US law, such as an LLM.

Attorneys who are admitted to practice in a state may engage in all aspects of criminal advocacy in that state. There is no "criminal bar" with separate requirements, although some states that still impose the **death penalty** may require a lawyer representing a defendant facing the penalty to demonstrate a high level of prior experience in the field.

B. ETHICAL DUTIES—GENERALLY

Each state adopts and enforces its own code of professional conduct, which is often based on (or at least similar to) the **Model Rules of Professional Conduct** promulgated by the American Bar Association. Each state will set up a disciplinary function that serves to enforce the state's rules of professional conduct. Some state disciplinary authorities will provide confidential advice to attorneys faced with an ethical dilemma about how to handle an ethical issue. These opinions are often published on an anonymized basis so that they can provide guidance to the members of the profession.

Among the professional duties and obligations to which attorneys are held responsible are the following:

- **Duty of care.** An attorney has an obligation to provide competent and diligent legal services commensurate with and responsive to the needs of the client or the organization by whom the attorney is retained. Particularly in the area of criminal law, an attorney should not represent a client if she does not have the skills and experience—and the available time—to do so competently; and once having agreed to represent a client, the attorney must do so energetically and diligently. In a criminal case, an attorney owes a duty of care to her client even if the client acknowledges, or the attorney is convinced of, guilt. The duty includes an obligation to search for evidence that may tend to exculpate the client, to diminish his responsibility, to diminish the significance of the alleged crime, or to bear on sentencing. An attorney must also proactively explore and evaluate, and discuss confidentially with the client, the possibility of a **negotiated outcome**, as noted in Chapter 11, and in the event of a conviction must pursue all appropriate steps to minimize the sentence that may be imposed. Failure to take professionally appropriate steps may, in egregious circumstances, lead to finding of **ineffective assistance of counsel** and can invalidate certain steps in a criminal matter if the attorney's unprofessional conduct caused prejudice to the client (see Chapter 9.C).
- Attorneys who are privately retained by clients are responsible for reaching an appropriate monetary arrangement with the client; once an attorney has agreed to represent a client and appears in court, and especially if trial is scheduled, a court may refuse to release an attorney from an obligation to provide a zealous defense to her client, even if the client refuses to pay her fees. A **contingency fee** where payment of the client's fees depends on the outcome of a criminal case is considered unethical.
- **Duty of loyalty.** An attorney must be sure that no other person's interest—including her own—interferes with her ability to provide competent legal advice or representation to a client. This includes a duty, rigorously enforced by courts and disciplinary committees, to avoid actual or potential conflicts of interest that may occur if the lawyer advises or represents two clients whose interests may conflict. When representing a client in a criminal matter, the attorney generally cannot represent another client in the same matter; while it may be

possible to do so if both clients provide informed and willing consent, such waivers must be carefully executed and will often be questioned by a judge or even the prosecutor, who may be concerned that the client may later disavow, on the basis of a conflict, decisions taken on the advice of an attorney who also represents someone else. If the attorney's fees are paid by anyone other than the client, the client's family, or (directly or indirectly) by the state if the defendant is unable to retain counsel, the attorney must be sure that the receipt of fees does not create an incentive to do anything other than provide the best possible defense for her client. Some corporations are obligated by their bylaws to provide legal representation to officers or employees who are investigated for acts committed within the apparent scope of their employment, sometimes on the condition that the fees be repaid if the individual is convicted.

- **Duty of confidentiality.** Communications between a client (including corporations) and an attorney are strictly covered by the **attorney/ client privilege**. This protection generally applies to someone who has not yet retained a lawyer but is speaking to one with the intention to do so. Absent the express consent of the client, the attorney can under no circumstances divulge to a third party information she has obtained from the client, or learned during the course of representing the client. If such privileged information is demanded by a prosecutor or another third party, an attorney must assert the privilege and refuse to answer. The attorney-client privilege applies to any substantive communications regarding legal advice to clients, and it also applies to an attorney's agents, such as assistants and paralegals. Privileged information can be **waived**, however, if a client discloses the privileged information himself, if the client authorizes the attorney to present information in court or to use in negotiation, or if a party puts privileged information at issue in litigation. For example, if a defendant argues that he relied on the advice of his counsel to unwittingly break the law and thereby lacked the requisite intent—often referred to as a **reliance on counsel defense**—he waives the privilege on that subject matter. This privilege generally applies to giving advice about, or representing a client concerning, the client's past conduct; if an attorney gives advice to a client that may be construed as advising the client on how to break the law in the future, the attorney may be viewed as an auxiliary of a criminal act, and may be forced to provide information about the advice under the so-called **crime fraud exception** to the privilege.

- A separate **work product doctrine** protects documents prepared in anticipation of litigation or for trial if they include or reflect the "mental impressions" or thinking of the attorney. The work product doctrine is less strictly enforced than the attorney/client privilege, and evidence falling under it is sometimes shared on a limited basis through **redaction,** or if another party can show hardship in the absence of obtaining it.

- **Duty of candor.** An attorney cannot make a false statement to a court, or introduce evidence known to be false, even if at the request or demand of a client. A very difficult situation arises if a client insists on testifying at trial under circumstances where the attorney objectively believes that the client's testimony will be false. An attorney's first obligation is to urge the client not to do so; in virtually all (but of course not all) instances, such advice is not only professionally appropriate but also strategically sound, since false testimony is in most instances likely to be discovered and lead to negative consequences, including an enhanced sentence in the event of conviction. On the particular issue of whether or not to testify, an attorney cannot bar a client from testifying, even on a belief that the testimony may be false; an attorney can, however, simply inform the court that the client wishes to testify without asking questions that elicit the false testimony.

- **Duty of honesty.** Lawyers must in general conduct themselves honestly, and in particular must scrupulously account for financial issues. Attorneys are permitted to set up **escrow accounts,** which are bank accounts in which they deposit money held for the benefit of, or belonging to, the client, and as to which the attorney becomes a fiduciary owing a strict duty to the client to account for the funds. Violations of that duty, which amount to theft, are very strictly punished.

If multiple individuals (or companies) are being investigated or preparing for a common trial, it is common for the attorneys representing them to work together. Normally, an attorney in such a situation could not share information obtained with her client with the attorney for another person (since doing so would violate the attorney/client privilege), and if a client were to share thoughts or information with another individual or company, or the attorney thereof, doing so might vitiate the privilege. In such a situation, it is common, and appropriate, for the parties and attorneys to reach a **joint defense agreement,** which recognizes the common interest among them, and allows the participants to share thoughts and information—and strategy—with others who join the agreement without breaching or waiving the attorney/client privilege. Such an agreement is based on the explicit assumption that all of its participants share the same general interest in opposing the prosecutor or other investigator. If a participant reaches an agreement with the prosecutor or investigator to **cooperate** by providing testimony or other evidence, he and his attorney must immediately cease participating in the joint meetings subject to the joint defense agreement and cannot share with the prosecutor or any other adverse party any information or evidence they learned through the operation of the joint defense agreement. Joint defense agreements are best reduced to writing.

C. ETHICAL DUTIES—THE PROSECUTION AND THE DEFENSE FUNCTIONS

Prosecutors and defense counsel share the same profession, and are both subject to the general ethical principles summarized here. But the profession also recognizes that their professional obligations may apply differently because of the nature of their responsibilities. These differences are clear in two sets of standards promulgated by the **American Bar Association** called, respectively, **Criminal Justice Standards for the Prosecution Function** and **Criminal Justice Standards for the Defense Function**. The standards for prosecutors emphasize that they are "administrators of justice," and that the prosecutor's duty is "to seek justice within the bounds of the law, and not merely to convict." The standards also emphasize that "in light of the prosecutor's public responsibilities, broad authority and discretion, the prosecutor has a heightened duty of candor to the courts and in fulfilling other professional obligations." The standards applicable to defense counsel note that "defense counsel have the difficult task of serving both as officers of the court and as loyal and zealous advocates for their clients." They thus provide that a defense lawyer cannot, even at the request or for the benefit of a client, violate the law or breach professional standards. In stark contrast to prosecutors, a defense counsel has only a "tempered duty of candor"; specifically, the duty of candor may "be tempered by competing ethical and constitutional obligations." The standards then specify that "defense counsel should not knowingly make a false statement of fact or law or offer false evidence, to a court, lawyer, witnesses, or third party.

It is not a false statement for defense counsel to suggest inferences that may reasonably be drawn from the evidence."

D. PENALTIES

Violations of professional rules may lead to a range of consequences:

- *Discipline of the attorney.* A client who feels that his attorney has failed to meet relevant professional standards may complain to the appropriate bar association or other entity responsible for disciplining attorneys in that state, and a judge may also refer the conduct to the applicable disciplinary authority for conduct that occurs in a matter she is supervising. In a disciplinary proceeding, the attorney will be provided with an opportunity to contest, explain, or minimize the conduct in question. Disciplinary penalties may include an admonition (sometimes public) by the disciplinary authority; temporary suspension for a period of time; or, in egregious cases, permanent disbarment.
- *Malpractice litigation.* While more common in civil litigation than in criminal matters, a client who believes that he has been harmed by his attorney's unprofessional conduct may contemplate suing the attorney for professional malpractice, which would take place in a separate civil proceeding.
- *Contempt.* Egregious misconduct occurring during a proceeding before a judge may cause the imposition of either of two kinds of a **contempt** citation. In so-called civil contempt, a judge may impose an immediate, on-the-spot sanction that in theory is designed to compel the attorney to comply with a court order or direction of the court, and which ceases upon compliance. "Criminal contempt" is in essence a separate criminal proceeding, where the attorney (or other participant in a proceeding) is charged with violating general rules or a specific order; punishment for criminal contempt does not lapse upon compliance with a court order. Contempt citations of either sort against attorneys in criminal cases are relatively infrequent and occur only in egregious circumstances.
- *Sanctions in the conduct of a criminal proceeding.* In some circumstances, misconduct by an attorney may result in the imposition of sanctions imposed by a court that are felt by the client. If an attorney fails to respect an obligation to share information with a prosecutor, for example, the court may bar the attorney from introducing evidence that should have been disclosed—even though doing so may hurt the client's defense.

- *Prosecution.* In extreme situations, especially concerning misuse of client or escrow funds that amounts to theft, an attorney may be prosecuted and held criminally responsible for her acts.
- *Ineffective assistance of counsel.* A client who feels that a negative outcome—such as a conviction or even a guilty plea—was the result of negligence of his attorney may try to undo the outcome (e.g., obtain a new trial, withdraw a guilty plea) by arguing that it was caused by unacceptably unprofessional conduct (as discussed previously in Chapter 9.C).

19 CONCLUSION

Is criminal justice in the United States all that different from criminal justice in other countries? The answer is clearly Yes. Defining conceptually the many ways how it differs is a complex, and perhaps academic, exercise. But given the increasing importance of transnational criminal investigations that compel prosecutors and others outside of the United States to deal with American procedures, it is becoming more and more urgent that the practical impact of these differences be understood.

Compared with the United Kingdom and countries whose legal traditions derive from it, the differences from US procedures may appear to be small. The United States shares not only the same language (and language is an extremely important component of law, as revealed by the challenges of translation) but also many important traditions derived from its English heritage; as a result, the vocabulary used in the two countries is often the same or similar. Chief among the similarities is the fact that both systems are based on trials before impartial lay juries, and that many of the procedures leading to and during trial—particularly prescriptive **rules of evidence**—reflect the centrality of jury decision-making. But either Oscar Wilde or George Bernard Shaw is said to have commented that the United States and the United Kingdom are two countries separated by a common language, and much the same could be said about British and American criminal law and procedures: the words often sound the same, but there are surprisingly important differences in how criminal justice is experienced in each country. An assumption by a practitioner in one country that she understands an analogous procedure in the other because of familiarity with the terminology may be partially—but only partially—correct, and may quickly lead to mistakes.

Differences between the two traditions that animate criminal justice in the United Kingdom and the United States, on the one hand, and in continental Europe, on the other (as well as the criminal justice cultures around the world that may have traditional links to one or another of these "families") are fundamental. Attempts to put these traditions into groups have resulted in a number of different classifications:

Common law	versus	Civil law
Common law based	versus	Code based
Adversarial	versus	Nonadversarial
Accusatorial	versus	Inquisitorial
Facts decided by juries	versus	Facts decided by judges
Prescriptive evidence rules	versus	Freedom of proof

All of these classifications inevitably oversimplify, and no single one survives much rigorous analysis. I nonetheless believe that core differences between the two approaches are in fact important and consequential.

In Europe, the prevailing belief is that a fair and neutral investigation should be able to establish, at least preliminarily, "the truth"—that is, "what really happened." The French Code of Criminal Procedure, for example, directs that a judge called an **investigating magistrate** should use all means available to "establish the truth" of a given situation—not as an advocate or prosecutor, but in the spirit of neutral inquiry, and in particular to track down and assemble all relevant evidence, whether incriminating or **exculpatory**. Once a preliminary conclusion has been reached that implicates a person as responsible for a criminal act, the trial serves to test whether this conclusion is sufficiently supported. In the Anglo/American approach, the "truth" may not be the touchstone of criminal justice so much as the concept of "fairness." In common law jurisdictions, the "truth" is not expected to be established by a neutral investigation but rather emerges from the presentation of contrasting narratives by adversarial parties (the prosecution and the defense) to a judge or (mostly) a jury, under procedures designed to protect fairness and in particular the right to an adequate defense. At the trial itself, the focus is less on figuring out "what happened" in the spirit of a neutral inquiry, and more on whether the prosecution has met a high **burden of proof** and overcome a strong **presumption of innocence** to support its accusation. As a result, an American trial is a public, intense, and highly proceduralized ritual that is carefully scrutinized on appeal for the essential fairness of the process rather than for the factual accuracy of its conclusion. And rather than a quasi-scientific or rationalist search for "the truth" based on all available inputs for whatever they may add, an Anglo/American trial is governed by strict, prescriptive **rules of evidence** where, in some instances, evidence that most people would consider useful in determining what happened is excluded to protect issues other than factual accuracy (for example, by excluding evidence seized in violation of the Constitution in order to deter police misconduct). In the spirit of fairness, an American defendant is not at all expected to contribute to an understanding of what happened and may—and often does—elect to rely on a right to silence, which at a European trial would be considered evidence of guilt.

A further important difference is the general principle in European legal systems (and legal cultures that derive from them) that no decision affecting a person's liberty or dignity should be made without a statement setting forth the reasons for the decision, which is capable of appropriate review. This is perhaps clearest with respect to the prosecutor's discretion whether to prosecute (or not), which in many European systems must be supported by a statement of reasons and may be reviewed by a judge if not made by one in the first instance. In stark contrast, as noted in Chapter 6.A, a US prosecutor does not need to give any explanation for a decision not to prosecute, and while in many instances a **grand jury** approval is necessary, the grand jury does not even purport to have reviewed all the potentially available evidence (there is no obligation to submit **exculpatory evidence** to a federal grand jury). Even after an indictment has issued with the approval of a grand jury, Rule 48(a) of the Federal Rules of Criminal Procedure, which provides that an indictment be **dismissed** at the request of the prosecutor and "with the approval of the court," has been universally interpreted to mean that a court has virtually no power to refuse to dismiss a pending indictment if a prosecutor so requests, for which she need give no reason.

Even more fundamentally, Americans historically view the institution of an independent lay **jury** as a centerpiece of our criminal justice system and a fundamental protection of individual rights. Jurors are classically nonstate actors, and it is not surprising that Americans tend to trust them more than state officials. But jury deliberations are also attractive precisely because the jurors are independent—they are *not* asked to explain their verdict, nor are in any way held accountable for it. In Europe, the European Court of Human Rights, interpreting the European Convention on Human Rights, has cast grave doubt about the validity of convictions based solely on verdicts by "lay juries" (that is, juries consisting only of nonprofessional citizens, as opposed to "mixed juries" that include both judges and jurors) because the verdicts are unexplained and incapable of review of their decision-making process or (in most instances) the accuracy of their fact-finding.

This book has attempted to explore in some detail the many procedures—often confusing to people not familiar with them and with the culture from which they sprang—that characterize American criminal justice. If we then take a step back and look at the procedural system as a whole, what themes appear—and, possibly, what lessons may be drawn?

As noted in the Introduction, the incidence of **guilty pleas** in the United States is strikingly high: about 95 percent of all criminal cases end in a guilty plea; in the federal system, the number now exceeds 97 percent. One might argue that such outcomes are presumptively rational: if the facts are clear to all concerned, what is the point of incurring the expense and disruption of a trial; why not save time, expense, and personal anguish by bypassing trial and going straight to the determination of a fair sentence based on the obvious facts? And in some—perhaps most—cases, the evidence in support of the prosecutor's case may be so strong that a trial would be virtually pointless. And guilty pleas are undeniably efficient, which may explain why other jurisdictions may be considering them.

But a number of distinctive aspects of American criminal justice strongly suggest that the rate of guilty pleas reflects an imbalance of power between prosecution and defense that is essentially built into the system, and has been exacerbated by some relatively recent developments.

Compared with counterparts in other countries, American prosecutors have a striking degree of independence, and of essentially
unreviewable power. The principle of **separation of the powers**—
which in the federal system reflects the allocation of power in the
Constitution between the executive and judicial branches—has been
interpreted by courts to mean that many decisions by prosecutors
cannot be reviewed by anyone else and do not need to be publicly
explained. At least in some procedural circumstances, only
a prosecutor—and not a judge—determines whether an outcome is
in the public interest. Even the appointment process puts little con-
straint on prosecutors: while federal prosecutors are named by the
President, strong traditions of independence not only protect them
from political interference but create little restraint or review of most
decisions; and in many state systems, prosecutors are locally elected
and thus have no hierarchical review at all. All prosecutors are virtually immune from personal accountability for their decisions.
US prosecutors can act quickly and nimbly in comparison with foreign counterparts, which may explain why they generally achieve far
more successful outcomes than their counterparts in multijurisdic-
tional investigations such as overseas bribery and money laundering.
They also have the freedom to be creative: To take a substantive
example, the US Congress has never defined the elements of the
crime of **insider trading** of publicly traded securities, yet over the
last few decades, federal prosecutors have achieved a remarkable
track record of successful prosecution by expansive interpretations
of generically written (and decades-old) antifraud statutes that do not
even mention insider trading as such. And on the side of procedure,
many corporate investigations now end in a **deferred prosecution
agreement**, described in Chapter 11.D. Congress has never authorized such practices, nor does any rule set forth the procedures for
them, but they have evolved at the hands of creative prosecutors—and
received not only a judicial imprimatur, but essentially a "hands-off"
response from the courts.

In the area of **guilty pleas**, the role of the prosecutor is pervasive.
In strict theory, and as set forth in Chapter 11.C, in the federal system
a judge is ultimately responsible for the imposition of sentence: the
prosecutor and the defense may agree on the position that the

prosecutor will take at sentence but must leave its imposition entirely up to the judge; or they may agree on a specific sentence, but with the explicit requirement that the judge can refuse to accept the plea if he determines that the sentence is inappropriate. In practice, prosecutors have huge control over sentencing. By tradition, it appears that judges simply give considerable, although certainly not controlling, weight to what prosecutors have to say. With the arrival of the **Federal Sentencing Guidelines** described in Chapter 14.B, prosecutorial impact on sentencing became more explicit (and powerful) for several reasons: Prosecutors can now appeal a sentence that they consider too low and may persuade an appellate court that the sentence imposed by the trial judge was "unreasonable." And further, the *only* means by which a defendant can escape scrutiny under the unforgiving matrix of the Guidelines is if the prosecutor, in her sole discretion, certifies that the defendant provided "cooperation" to the prosecution.

The growth of **mandatory minimum sentences**, explored in Chapter 14.B, further enhances prosecutorial power in ways probably not contemplated by legislative drafters. The theory of mandatory sentencing is to reduce the exercise of discretion by judges and prose-cutors, ostensibly to cut back on perceived disparities in the imposition of sentencing, but implicitly to increase the length of sentences. The mandatory regime accomplishes this by creating certain nominally objective criteria that, if present, obligate both the prosecutor to seek and the judge to impose minimum sentences. Some of the objective criteria are matters of record, such as the number and quality of prior convictions that may signal a recidivist. Other criteria, however, are theoretically factual—but critically depend not on what "actually hap-pened" but on the *facts that the prosecutor chooses to charge*. In the area of narcotics, for example, the applicability of mandatory minimum sen-tences depends not only on the kind but also the amount of narcotics for which the defendant is charged with responsibility—which may not be the same as the amount of narcotics actually involved. During the presidency of Barack Obama, the Department of Justice commendably attempted to cut back on the country's burgeoning prison population by urging prosecutors to not automatically charge all of the narcotics revealed by an investigation, but in circumstances such as a first offen-der or in the absence of violence, to charge only a lesser amount of the actual narcotics seized so that the mandatory minimum upon conviction would either be lower or not applicable at all. While the impetus for this approach was commendable, it nonetheless creates a jurisprudential anomaly that would be impossible in many other countries: rather than based upon an objective "truth" in the sense of *what really happened*, the determination of the sentence depends critically on a unilateral, unreviewable decision by a prosecutor about *what to charge*: If a prosecutor elects (or negotiates) to diminish the factual allegations against a defendant, then that defendant has at least a chance of a relatively lower sentence; but if *even based on the exactly same facts* the prosecutor elects to charge the full quantity actually seized, in the event of conviction the judge is without power to impose a sentence below the (often quite high) minimum.

When such unreviewable power to control critical factual parameters is put in the hands of prosecutors, it inevitably leads to a disparity in bargaining power in the **negotiation** of non-trial outcomes. As noted in the discussion of **guilty pleas** in Chapter 11.C, prosecutors can—and do—negotiate over whether the defendant will agree to **waive** his rights. Any plea, by definition, includes a waiver of the right to go to trial, and a judge contemplating a proffered guilty plea under **Rule 11** must make it clear on the record that the defendant understands this. See Chapter 11.C.1. What may *not* be on the record, however, is a prior explicit or implicit negotiation where the prosecutor may have offered to reduce the *factual* allegations against the defendant (along the lines suggested during the Obama administration in an effort to stem the increase in prison populations) but *only* if the defendant agreed to plead guilty—or if the defendant agreed not to make motions, including **motions to suppress**, as discussed in Chapter 10.C. One can easily hypothesize, then, a situation where a defendant may believe that he has a good argument that key evidence against him was seized in violation of the Constitution or applicable laws, and that he might obtain a favorable ruling suppressing the evidence from use at trial by making such a motion. Given the prosecutor's control over the factual charges against him, however, he may also know that even by making such a motion to assert his rights, he will have lost an opportunity to bargain with the prosecutor to charge him with responsibility for less than all of the facts supported

by the evidence—and thereby avoid the risk of a high mandatory
minimum sentence if convicted. In essence, by allowing
a prosecutor unilaterally to determine factual parameters, the prosecutor can—and sometimes does—put a huge cost on the exercise of
constitutional and other rights, and there is no way for a defendant to
ask a judge to review this. As noted in Chapter 14.C, the **First Step
Act** that became law in December 2018 may add some new flexibility
to federal mandatory minimum sentencing regimes, notably by
increasing the potential applicability of so-called **safety valves** that
may allow certain limited categories of defendants to escape the rigors
of automatic, rigid, and mandatory minimum sentences. As already
noted, the changes are welcome but modest, and it will take some time
to determine their impact on actual sentences. They do not appear to
be of a magnitude that will affect the principal dynamics of plea
negotiation or change the disproportionate power exercised by
prosecutors.

In addition, while defendants have certain very specific rights—
discussed in Chapter 10.B—to **discover** the evidence against them,
some of those discovery rights arise only in anticipation of (or even
during) a trial; the right of a defendant to know all the evidence against
him as a prerequisite to plea negotiations is currently the subject of
considerable discussion, but is hardly seamless. And if a defendant
pleads guilty, he may be asked to expressly waive the right to claim
that he had not been provided with adequate access to the evidence
against him that he used as a basis to decide to plead guilty.

The result of these phenomena is set forth in Figures 1, 2, and 3 in
the Introduction: while the number of trials has decreased to less than
3 percent of all criminal matters in the federal system, the number of
individuals in prison has mushroomed, to a point that puts the United
States literally in a class by itself when compared with other economically advanced countries.

The decreasing incidence of trials also leads to a view—hard to
establish empirically, but convincing to this author among many
others—that as guilty plea outcomes increasingly become a default,
all participants in the system may become institutionally lazy. For
a prosecutor, why not "overcharge"—charge more serious crimes
than the evidence necessarily supports—when the enhanced charge is

unlikely ever to be tested in court, but might be useful in negotiation? Such a mind-set is deeply pernicious: at its most basic level, the core theory of the "adversarial" system of justice is precisely to keep prosecutors honest through the knowledge that whatever they may choose to allege or do, their decisions and acts are subject to being tested at trial by an equally talented and motivated adversary. But this check on prosecutorial discretion diminishes as the likelihood of trials recedes. As a result, the US criminal justice system is increasingly characterized by unusually complex, cumbersome procedures, often capable of manipulation or unfairness, derived from an adversarial tradition based on the assumption that a trial will eventually take place, even though the trials upon which these procedures depend for their fundamental functionality, validity, and fairness are becoming vanishingly scarce.

A further consideration is how fundamentally complicated, risky, consequential, and unpredictable the American jury trial has grown to be. Particularly because they result in "all or nothing" outcomes with wildly different consequences, it is perhaps little wonder that participants may be tempted to avoid the risks associated with them in favor of an imperfect but predictable compromise. Trials can also be hugely expensive and resource-consuming. It was recently reported that a single individual defendant in a federal criminal trial expended more than US$30 million in legal defense costs. Such expenditures raise troubling questions about the adequacy of legal justice available to defendants with fewer or no resources. But when I mention this figure to non-US audiences, they often have another question as well: How on earth could anyone manage to run up such expenses in a single trial? The answer is that what jurors actually see and hear at trial may be the tip of the proverbial iceberg—the final battle of a lengthy, intense, multifronted war where each side attempts to "control the narrative" presented at trial. The jury may end up spending only a few weeks or even a few days hearing the evidence that survives the onslaught of adversarial pretrial motions and the filter of prescriptive evidentiary rules to be deemed admissible at trial, but their role only happens after (and is invisibly shaped by) sometimes herculean efforts by each side to develop factual and expert testimony in their favor, and to hinder the ability of the adversary to present a contrary narrative. Even a relatively

simple trial strains the resources of the participants, particularly prosecutors' offices and the offices of defense counsel paid by the state to
represent the indigent; many of the latter are already swamped beyond
their ability to provide professionally competent defenses to the people
who need them. As noted in Chapter 11.C relating to **guilty pleas**, one
reason for their prevalence, and in particular for a near-universal "plea
discount" of a reduced sentence for anyone who pleads guilty, is that
even a modest increase in the number of trials would put a burden on
already scarce resources (and, as a politically sensitive matter, increase
government budgets), which leads to an uncomfortable conclusion that
the complexity and resource-intensity of criminal trials puts a big
burden on the exercise of constitutional rights.

From a purely rationalist perspective, an adversarial system
designed around the theoretically (but increasingly unlikely) possibility
of jury trial might not be a candidate for an optimum process to decide
guilt. As noted in Chapter 10.C, during the pretrial phase of
a complicated case in the United States, the adversaries are to some
degree engaged in a "chess match" dedicated not so much to "establishing the truth" in any neutral or objective sense but to improving
their strategic position at trial, often by depriving the adversary of
potential arguments or evidence, even if the evidence bears directly
on guilt. The jurors may not really reflect a "cross section of the
community," but may have been (unbeknownst to themselves)
selected by parties armed with insights from sophisticated juror profiling. During the trial the jurors, who by definition know nothing of the
case before the trial starts, are allowed to ask virtually no questions (and
then only during deliberation, when all the evidence has been presented); their understanding of facts is tightly constrained by rules of
evidence and other limitations, such that admissibility (that is, what the
jurors actually learn about) is not exclusively determined by propensity
for accuracy. They ultimately decide a single question—guilty or not
guilty—without giving any basis for (nor facing any fear of being
questioned about) their answer, which can be reviewed on appeal for
the regularity of the procedures that led to it, but fundamentally not for
the key question that the jury was asked to decide: Was the defendant in
fact guilty? It is hard to imagine any rational person devising this model
as the best one for making important decisions in life, and it is thus not

surprising that many outside observers do not find American criminal procedures to be fair or just. But because of history and culture, that is how "justice" is conceived in the United States.

In many circumstances, of course, the American system of justice really does work: Both the abundant television and written fiction about investigations and trials, but also history, reveal countless instances where a determined defense lawyer was able to ferret out hidden evidence, often obscured by official laziness or worse, and averted a miscarriage of justice. The presumption of innocence at all times, the right to confront (and cross examine) all witnesses, a right to silence not only before but at trial, and perhaps most importantly a healthy skepticism about "official versions" of the truth are understandably critical to American criminal justice values. And because jurors are nonstate actors—and not officials—their verdicts tend to be accepted. A slimmed down process such as trials in continental Europe would certainly be cheaper, and in some ways may be more rational, than their American counterparts, but they would never satisfy an American sense of whether "justice has been done" because they do not reflect some core American values. What I hope this book demonstrates is that those values may be slipping away as trials disappear and plea negotiations increasingly become one-sided.

A final word: As noted in the Introduction, American criminal justice is undeniably marred by issues of race, class, and unequal access to resources. The impact on many communities of the extraordinary high level of incarceration—far higher than in other economically advanced countries—is profound. Statistics relating not only to prison populations but also to incidence of arrests tend strongly to show that the proportion of those arrested as well as those convicted falls disproportionately on racial minorities. The death penalty is in the view of many, including this author, profoundly unjust, not only because of the small but unacceptable and absolutely inevitable risk that innocent defendants will be executed, but because race is such an important factor (particularly with respect to the race of the victim, since statistics show that a person convicted of killing a white person is far more likely to be sentenced to death than a person convicted of killing a black person). Austerity measures in many communities have cut back on the resources available for criminal justice, especially budgets available to fund an adequate defense for indigents accused of crime. This book cannot explore these extremely important—in fact, urgent—issues; some of the excellent works cited in the Bibliography do. But understanding the procedural environment in which these and other anomalies occur is, I believe, necessary to addressing them.

BIBLIOGRAPHY

I. PRIMARY SOURCES

A. Federal

Constitution of the United States of America, available at www.constitution
.findlaw.com/.
Federal Criminal Code, 18 U.S. C. § 1 et seq, available at www.law.cornell
.edu/usco de/text/18.
Bail Reform Act of 1984, 18 U.S.C. §§ 3141–50 (2018).
Jencks Act, 18 U.S.C. § 3500 (2018).
Sentencing Reform Act of 1984, 18 U.S.C. §§ 3551–59 (2018).
Speedy Trial Act of 1974, 18 U.S.C. §§ 3161–62, 3164 (2018).
Stored Communications Act, 18 U.S.C. §§ 2701–12 (2018).
Federal Rules of Criminal Procedure (2018), www.federalrulesofcriminal
procedure.org/.
Federal Rules of Appellate Procedure (2018), www.federalrulesofappella
teprocedure.org/ table-of-contents/.
Federal Rules of Evidence (2018), www.rulesofevidence.org/.
Rules of the Supreme Court of the United States (2017), www
.supremecourt.gov/ filingandrules/ 2017RulesoftheCourt.pdf.
Federal Sentencing Guidelines Manual (2016), www.ussc.gov/guidelines/
2016-guidelines-manual.

B. New York State

New York State Constitution, available at www.dos.ny.gov/info/constitution
.htm.

New York Penal Law (Consol. 2017), available at www.ypdcrime.com/
penal.law/.
New York State Criminal Procedure Law (Consol. 2017), available at www
.ypdcrime.com/cpl/.
Guide to New York Evidence, www.nycourts.gov/judges/evidence/
1-GENERAL/1-generalprovisions.shtml.

II. OVERVIEWS

Bradley, Craig M., ed. *Criminal Procedure: A Worldwide Study.* 2nd ed.
Durham, NC: Carolina Academic Press, 2007.
Chemerinsky, Erwin, and Levenson, Laurie. *Criminal Procedure.* 3rd ed.
New York: Wolters Kluwer, 2017.
Dressler, Joshua, et al. *Understanding Criminal Procedure. Vol. 1: Investigation.*
Durham, NC: Carolina Academic Press, 2017.
Dressler, Joshua, et al. *Understanding Criminal Procedure. Vol. 2: Adjudication.*
Durham, NC: Carolina Academic Press, 2017.
Israel, Jerold, et al. *Criminal Procedure and the Constitution: Leading
Supreme Court Cases and Introductory Text.* St. Paul, MN: West
Academic Publishing, 2017.
Kamisar, Yale, et al. *Advanced Criminal Procedure.* 14th ed. St. Paul, MN:
West Academic Publishing, 2015.
Kamisar, Yale, et al. *Basic Criminal Procedure.* 14th ed. St. Paul, MN: West
Academic Publishing, 2015.
Kamisar, Yale, et al. *Modern Criminal Procedure: Cases, Comments, and
Questions.* St. Paul, MN: West Academic Publishing, 2015.
Model Penal Code. Philadelphia: American Law Institute, 1962.
Organization of American States. *Guide to Criminal Prosecutions in the
United States.* Washington, DC: 2007.
Worrall, John L. *Criminal Procedure: From First Contact to Appeal.* 6th ed.
Boston: Pearson, 2018.

III. FEDERALISM AND CRIMINAL LAW

Barkow, Rachel E. "Federalism and Criminal Law: What the Feds Can
Learn from the States." *Mich. L. R.* 109, no. 4 (2011), 519–580.
Fallon, Richard, et al. *Hart and Wechsler's The Federal Courts and the
Federal System.* 7th ed. St. Paul, MN: Foundation Press, 2015.

Fissell, Brenner. "Federalism and Constitutional Criminal Law." *Hofstra L. R.* 46, no. 489 (2018), 489–562.

Klein, Susan R. "Independent-Norm Federalism in Criminal Law." *Cal. L.R.* 90, no. 5 (2002), 1541–1592.

Richman, Daniel, and Stith, Kate. *Defining Federal Crimes.* New York: Wolters Kluwer, 2019.

IV. INVESTIGATION AND EVIDENCE GATHERING

Clancy, Thomas K. *The Fourth Amendment: Its History and Interpretation.* 3rd ed. Durham, NC: Carolina Academic Press, 2017.

Hess Orthmann, Christine, and Hess, Kären M. *Criminal Investigation.* 10th ed. Boston: Cengage Learning, 2012.

LaFave, Wayne R. *Search and Seizure: A Treatise on the Fourth Amendment.* 5th ed. St. Paul, MN: Thomson West, 2012.

V. PRETRIAL ISSUES

A. General

Allen, Ronald J., et al. *Criminal Procedure: Investigation & Right to Counsel.* 3rd ed. New York: Wolters Kluwer, 2016.

Davis, Angela J. *Arbitrary Justice: The Power of the American Prosecutor.* New York: Oxford University Press, 2009.

Wadhia, Shoba Sivaprasad. *Beyond Deportation: The Role of Prosecutorial Discretion in Immigration Cases.* New York: New York University Press, 2015.

B. Discovery

Cary, Robert M., et al. *Federal Criminal Discovery.* Chicago: ABA Book Publishing, 2011.

Cline, Richard. *Defense Investigation and Discovery in Criminal Cases: A Systematic Approach to Obtaining Information and Preparing for Trial.* St. Paul, MN: Thomson Reuters, 2011.

Moisidis, Cosmas. *Criminal Discovery: From Truth to Proof and Back Again.* Sydney: Federation Press, 2008.

C. Plea Negotiation

Alschuler, Albert W. "Plea Bargaining and Its History." *Columbia Law Review* 79 (1979), 1–43.

Fisher, George, *Plea Bargaining's Triumph: A History of Plea Bargaining in America.* Stanford, CA: Stanford University Press, 2004.

Garrett, Brandon L. "Why Plea Bargains Are Not Confessions," *William & Mary L. Rev.* 57, no. 4 (2016), 1415–1444.

Heumann, Milton. *Plea Bargaining: The Experiences of Prosecutors, Judges, and Defense Attorneys.* Chicago: University of Chicago Press, 1977.

Petegorsky, Michael Nasser. "Plea Bargaining in the Dark: The Duty to Disclose Exculpatory Brady Evidence during Plea Bargaining." *Fordham L. Rev.* 81, no. 6 (2013), 3599–3650.

Schulhofer, Stephen J. "Is Plea Bargaining Inevitable?" *Harvard Law Review* 97, no. 5 (1984), 1037–1107.

Vogel, Mary E. *Coercion to Compromise: Plea Bargaining, the Courts and the Making of Political Authority.* Oxford: Oxford University Press, 2007.

D. Motion Practice

Adams, James A., and Blinka, Daniel D. *Pretrial Motions in Criminal Prosecutions.* 4th ed. New York: LexisNexis, 2008.

E. Speedy Trial

Herman, Susan N. *The Right to a Speedy and Public Trial: A Reference Guide to the United States Constitution.* 3rd ed. Santa Barbara, CA: Praeger, 2006.

VI. TRIALS AND EVIDENCE

Abramson, Jeffrey. *We, the Jury: The Jury System and the Ideal of Democracy Rights.* Cambridge, MA: Harvard University Press, 2000.

Banaszak, Ronald, ed. *Fair Trial Rights of the Accused: A Documentary History.* Westport, CT: Greenwood Press, 2001.

Brodin, Mark S., et al. *Weinstein's Federal Evidence: Commentary on Rules of Evidence for the United States Courts.* 2nd ed. New York: LexisNexis, 2018.

Broun, Kenneth S., et al. *McCormick on Evidence*. 7th ed. St. Paul, MN: West Academic Publishing, 2014.

Fisher, George. *Evidence*. 3rd ed. New York: Foundation Press, 2012.

Lieberman, Joel D., and Krauss, Daniel A. *Jury Psychology: Social Aspects of Trial Processes*, Vol. 1. New York: Routledge, 2016.

Lubet, Steven. *Modern Trial Advocacy: Analysis and Practice*. 4th ed. LexisNexis, 2009.

New York Criminal Jury Instructions and Model Colloquies. New York State Unified Court System. www.nycourts.gov/judges/cji/2-PenalLaw/cji3.shtml.

Saltzburg, Stephen A., et al. *Federal Rules of Evidence Manual*. 11th ed. New Providence, NJ: LexisNexis, 2015.

Siffert, John S. *Modern Federal Jury Instructions*. New Providence, NJ: LexisNexis, 2018.

Sklansky, David A. *Evidence: Cases, Commentary, and Problems*. 4th ed. New York: Wolters Kluwer, 2015.

Spencer, JR. *Hearsay Evidence in Criminal Proceedings*. 2nd ed. Portland, OR: Hart Publishers, 2014.

VII. SENTENCING

Alexander, Michelle. *The New Jim Crow: Mass Incarceration in the Age of Colorblindness*. New York: The New Press, 2010.

Alschuler, Albert W. "The Failure of Sentencing Guidelines: A Plea for Less Aggregation." *University of Chicago Law Review* 58 (1993), 901–951.

Bierschbach, Richard A., and Bibas, Stephanos. "What's Wrong with Sentencing Equality." *Virginia Law Review* 102, no. 6 (2016), 1447–1522.

Cassidy, R. Michael, and Ullmann, Robert L. "Sentencing Reform: The Power of Reasons." *Massachusetts Law Review* 97, no. 4 (2016), 80–83.

Demleitner, Nora, and Berman, Douglas A. *Sentencing Law and Policy*. New York: Wolters Kluwer, 2018.

Freed, Daniel J. "Federal Sentencing in the Wake of Guidelines: Unacceptable Limits on the Discretion of Sentencers." *Yale Law Journal* 101 (1992), 1681–1754.

Mitchell, Kelly Lyn. "State Sentencing Guidelines: A Garden Full of Variety." *Federal Probation* 81, no. 2 (2017), 28–36.

Morris, Norval, and Tonry, Michael. *Between Prison and Probation: Intermediate Punishments in a Rational Sentencing System.* New York: Oxford University Press, 1991.

Sidhu, Dawinder S. "Towards the Second Founding of Federal Sentencing." *Maryland Law Review* 77, no. 2 (2018), 485–546.

Stith, Kate, and Cabranes José A. *Fear of Judging: Sentencing Guidelines in the Federal Courts.* Chicago: University of Chicago Press, 1998.

Tonry, Michael. *Sentencing Matters.* New York: Oxford University Press, 1996.

United States Sentencing Commission. 2017 Sourcebook of Federal Sentencing Statistics. www.ussc.gov/research/sourcebook-2017.

VIII. APPEALS AND COLLATERAL ATTACKS

Garrett, Brandon, and Kovarsky, Lee. *Federal Habeas Corpus: Executive Detention and Post-conviction Litigation.* St. Paul, MN: Foundation Press, 2013.

Lyon, Andrea D., et al. *Federal Habeas Corpus: Cases and Materials.* 2nd ed. Durham, NC: Carolina Academic Press, 2011.

Schapiro, Stephen M., et al. *Supreme Court Practice.* 10th ed. New York: Bloomberg BNA, 2013.

IX. PROFESSIONAL RESPONSIBILITY IN CRIMINAL MATTERS

American Bar Association. Criminal Justice Standards for the Defense Function (2015). www.americanbar.org/groups/criminal_justice/stan dards/DefenseFunctionFourthEdition-TableofContents.html.

American Bar Association. Criminal Justice Standards for the Prosecution Function (2015). www.americanbar.org/groups/criminal_justice/stan dards/ProsecutionFunctionFourthEdition-TableofContents.html.

Berger, Todd A. "Professional Responsibility of the Criminal Defense Lawyer Redux: The New Three Hardest Questions." *St. Mary's J. on Legal Malpractice & Ethics* 7, no. 2 (2017), 96–159.

Gillers, Stephen. *Regulation of Lawyers: Problems of Law and Ethics.* 11th ed. New York: Wolters Kluwer, 2018.

Murray, Brian M. "Prosecutorial Responsibility and Collateral Consequences." *Stan. J. C.R. & C.L.* 12, no. 2 (2016), 213–248.

Swisher, Keith. "The Judicial Ethics of Criminal Law Adjudication."
Arizona State Law Journal 41, no. 3 (Fall 2009), 755–828.

X. COMPARATIVE AND CRITICAL PERSPECTIVES

Bettwy, Samuel W. *Comparative Criminal Procedure through Film:
Analytical Tools and Law and Film Summaries by Legal Tradition and
Country.* Lake Mary, FL: Vandeplas, 2015.

Bradley, Craig M. ed. *Criminal Procedure: A Worldwide Study.* 2nd ed.
Durham, NC: Carolina Academic Press, 2007.

Burns, Robert P. *The Death of the American Trial.* Chicago: University of
Chicago Press, 2011.

Damaška, Mirjan R. *Evidence Law Adrift.* Repr. ed. New Haven: Yale
University Press, 2013.

Damaška, Mirjan R. *The Faces of Justice and State Authority: A Comparative
Approach to the Legal Process.* New Haven: Yale University Press, 1986.

Eisinger, Jesse. *The Chickenshit Club: Why the Justice Department Fails to
Prosecute Executives.* New York: Simon & Schuster, 2017.

Garapon, Antoine, and Papadopoulos, Ioannis. *Juger en Amérique et en
France.* Paris: Odile Jacob, 2003.

Garrett, Brandon L. *End of Its Rope: How Killing the Death Penalty Can
Revive Criminal Justice.* Cambridge, MA: Harvard University Press,
2017.

Garrett, Brandon L. *Too Big to Jail: How Prosecutors Compromise with
Corporations.* New York: Belknap Press, 2014.

Garrett, Brandon L. *Convicting the Innocent.* Cambridge, MA: Harvard
University Press, 2011.

Jackson, John D., and Summers, Sarah J. *The Internationalisation of
Criminal Evidence: Beyond the Common Law and Civil Law Traditions.*
New York: Cambridge University Press, 2012.

Jouet, Mugambi. *Exceptional America: What Divides Americans from the
Rest of the World and from Each Other.* Oakland, CA: University of
California Press, 2017.

Langer, Maximo, and Sklansky, David Alan, eds. *Prosecutors and
Democracy, A Cross-National Study.* Cambridge, UK: Cambridge
University Press, 2017.

Pakes, Francis J. *Comparative Criminal Justice.* 3rd ed. New York:
Routledge, Taylor and Francis Group, 2015.

Roach, Kent. "Wrongful Convictions: Adversarial and Inquisitorial Themes." *35 N.C.J. Inter'l & Com. Reg.* 387 (2009).

Ross, Jacqueline E., and Thaman Stephen C., eds. *Comparative Criminal Procedure*. Northampton, MA: Edward Elgar Publishing, 2016.

The Secret Barrister, *The Secret Barrister: Stories of the Law and How It's Broken*. London: Macmillan, 2018.

Stevenson, Bryan. *Just Mercy: A Story of Justice and Redemption*. New York: Spiegal & Grau, 2014.

Thaman, Stephen C. *Comparative Criminal Procedure: A Casebook Approach*. 2nd ed. Durham, NC: Carolina Academic Press, 2008.

Thaman, Stephen C. *Exclusionary Rules in Comparative Law*. New York: Springer, 2013.

Thaman, Stephen. *World Plea Bargaining: Consensual Procedures and the Avoidance of the Full Criminal Trial*. Durham, NC: Carolina Academic Press, 2010.

Turner, Jenia I. *Plea Bargaining Across Borders: Criminal Procedure*. New York: Aspen Publishers, 2010.

Whitman, James Q. *Harsh Justice: Criminal Punishment and the Widening Divide between America and Europe*. New York: Oxford University Press, 2005.

INDEX